Elizabeth Mayo, Charles Mayo, Robert Dunning

Pestalozzi and His Principles

Elizabeth Mayo, Charles Mayo, Robert Dunning

Pestalozzi and His Principles

ISBN/EAN: 9783337311773

Printed in Europe, USA, Canada, Australia, Japan

Cover: Foto ©Suzi / pixelio.de

More available books at **www.hansebooks.com**

PESTALOZZI

AND HIS PRINCIPLES.

FOURTH EDITION, REVISED.

PUBLISHED FOR THE HOME AND COLONIAL SCHOOL SOCIETY
AT THE DEPOSITORY, GRAY'S INN ROAD, W.C.

SIM IN, MARSHALL, HAMILTON, KENT AND CO.,
PATERNOSTER ROW, E.C.

1890.

PART I.

A LECTURE ON THE LIFE OF

PESTALOZZI.

BY THE

REV. C. MAYO, LL.D.,

Fellow of St. John's College, Oxford.

WITH NOTES, ORIGINAL AND SELECTED,

By ROBERT DUNNING,

LECTURER ON SCHOOL MANAGEMENT, HOME AND COLONIAL
TRAINING COLLEGE.

MEMOIR OF PESTALOZZI.

SOME years ago, an Irish gentleman travelling through Yverdon, in the Pays de Vaud, was prevailed on to spend a couple of hours in the Institution of Pestalozzi.* The first class he inspected was carried on in

* The "Irish gentleman" here referred to is, no doubt, Mr. Mills, so long the intelligent, active Principal of the old Kildare Place Institution in Dublin. He wrote a sketch of Pestalozzi's "Intuitive System of Calculation," which contains a clear exposition of the principles of Pestalozzi, applied to the teaching of mental arithmetic, by one of his coadjutors, Hermann Krusi. He also introduced Krusi's "Tables of the Relations of Numbers" into the Model Schools in Dublin, and taught their use to all Irish teachers sent up to be trained. It was the means of infusing for a time great life into many of the Irish schools in connection with the teaching of number; although with imperfectly instructed teachers it degenerated into a mere mechanical process. The same tables were introduced into this country by Sir J. K. Shuttleworth and Mr. Tufnell, and, under the auspices of the Council of Educatior, an attempt was made to diffuse a knowledge of the method of working them among London teachers. The effort was, however, unsuccessful, either from the profession not being prepared to receive them, or from their indiscriminate use at all stages of progress, or from not making them sufficiently inductive as well as

B

a language not familiar to him ; yet was he much
struck with the intelligence and vivacity portrayed in

intuitive, as they were intended to be. By the younger Krusi, for
some years a teacher in our Institution, they were handled with
great spirit. He made the teaching, in the first place, intuitive and
inductive, and when he had arrived at a general truth, and for-
mulated it, he reversed the operation, proceeding deductively, using
abstract numbers. The effect was, that not only were the relations
of numbers seen, and the power of calculation obtained, but the
mind of the pupil was kept in healthy and moderate exercise. Still,
Krusi's method is not equal to that introduced by Mr. Reiner,
another disciple of Pestalozzi, in his "Lessons on Number." A
complete system of mental arithmetic is elaborated, carrying the
child from the perception of unity in connection with objects through
all the elementary operations of whole numbers—fractions, square
numbers, and proportion. It is a different thing from the mental
arithmetic of our common school treatises, and goes beyond the
tables of Krusi in cultivating more mental power, and avoiding
everything mechanical. Very good expositions of Krusi's method
were given in the "Traveller's Sketch," and in a treatise published
under the sanction of the Privy Council in 1844 ; both are out of
print. For the method of Reiner, see his "Master's Manual" and
"Praxis." Tait's "First Principles of Arithmetic" is a mixture of
Krusi and Reiner, with additional exercises of a varied kind, applied
to business calculations, but neither as well graduated nor giving
the systematic exercise of mind afforded by Reiner. The exclusion
of Krusi's tables from our schools is to be regretted, as by a skilful
teacher they might be used with great advantage, especially in
aiding the weak and backward, and at the first stage of each elementary process. The want of discrimination and skill in their application have been the blight of the best discoveries and inventions that
genius has bestowed on education. Sometimes the fault has been

the features of the pupils.* But when he witnessed
the power of the method in its application to arith-

with the inventor in presenting that as general in its application
which was only of partial application, and sometimes with the
operator who does not know the special circumstances of its application. It is as important to know the where, the when, and the
how as the *what* of a method. It is enough to lack the spirit of the
originator, but worse to mistake the scope and power of his work.
It is to be hoped that Krusi's tables will yet get a place among the
apparatus of a school, and be appreciated as they deserve.

* The intelligence and vivacity which arrested the attention of the
visitor were better proofs of the excellence of the methods of Pestalozzi than any mere proficiency in the elements of learning and
readiness of memory in the repetition of tasks. He showed the
practised eye of the intelligent educationalist, in appreciating the
best part of education—its influence on the mind, and in detecting
at the same time the character of the methods used by their surest
signs. The teaching of Pestalozzi addresses the intelligence of the
pupil at its lowest stage; next brings his intellectual faculties into a
state of activity, and after this excites his sympathy and interest, so
as to give vivacity and pleasure in learning. Thus not only is
intellectual progress secured, but intellectual tastes and habits are
formed—education, not mere instruction, takes place. For several
years the whole current of public opinion and governmental superintendence set in against intelligent teaching. The instruments of
knowledge—reading, writing, and arithmetic—received undue if not
exclusive attention, and were taught and examined in the most
mechanical manner possible. A new era has dawned : henceforth,
as stamped by the voice of authority, intelligence at least shall be
cultivated in connection with arithmetic. See the instructions given
to the Inspectors of Schools. This, conjoined with the teaching of
the " higher subjects " and the examination of pupils on the purport

B 2

metic, he discovered in the scholars a clear conception
of number and its relations, a precision and rapidity
in mental calculation, an animation and an interest in
their employment, which convinced him that a secret
had been discovered by Pestalozzi ; and he resolved,
if possible, to penetrate it.* His proposed visit of

of what is read, will make intelligence more general, and no doubt
facilitate the adoption of the methods if not of the principles of
Pestalozzi.

  * The main object of Pestalozzi's instruction was the development
of the mental powers ; and this he accomplished with so much
success, that the ability of his pupils displayed in mental arithmetic
was one of the chief means of attracting the attention of the public
to his experiments.   Pestalozzianism has often since been judged by
the excellency of its arithmetical teaching.   On the other hand,
whether a teacher understands and applies the principles of Pestalozzi may be readily known by the character and results of the
teaching in this branch of knowledge.   It can be easily seen
whether he has only reached an explanatory method or arrived at
that of developing power.   The general inferiority of the arithmetic
in our public elementary schools, as reported by H.M. Inspectors,
does not arise, I believe, so much from the comparative difficulty of
the subject as from the mechanical method by which it is taught.
In the training of the students here we experience much difficulty in
making them feel the importance and prior claim of mental arithmetic, and thus in cultivating mental power.   In teaching it we are
preparing for higher practical results.   But to return to Pestalozzi :
it is difficult which to admire most, the methods by which he gal-
vanized a dead body into life, or the sagacity that selected a subject
pre-eminently calculated to produce all the phenomena witnessed by
the traveller—"clearness of conception," " precision and rapidity

two hours terminated at the expiration of three months; nor was his admiration of the method confined to a bare speculative reception of the principles. He transplanted into his own country the practical truths he had learned in Switzerland; and, though Providence has interrupted the course of his more extended labours, he still, in the bosom of his own family, applies the lessons of Pestalozzi, and teaches his children to revere the name. It was not a theoretical examination of the method that effected this conviction and animated to these exertions; it was a

of thought," and "animation and interest." Dr. Mayo observes on the point, in his Introduction to " Lessons on Number" :—" Number presents a most important field, on which to develop and strengthen the minds of children. Its obvious connection with the circumstances surrounding them—the simplicity of its data—the clearness and certainty of its processes—the neatness and indisputable correctness of its results—adapt it in an eminent degree for early instruction. Arithmetical exercises tend to give clearness, activity, and tenacity to the mind; many an intellect that has not power enough for geometry, nor refinement enough for language, finds in them a department of study on which it may labour with the invigorating consciousness of success. But the advantages must of course depend on the manner in which arithmetic is taught. More than any other branch of instruction has it suffered, in this country, from the influence of circumstances. The reproach that we are a nation of shopkeepers might seem to have originated in the spirit of our arithmetical studies." Pestalozzi seized the subject as a fit instrument of mental culture, and his disciples have furnished us with admirable methods of turning it to the best advantage.

personal view of the practical influence of the system, in scenes lit up by the genius and warmed with the benevolence of Pestalozzi himself.

Could I transport you in thought to the scenes where he lived, and taught, and suffered, with his scholars, the heart would feel, even before the understanding discerned, the beauty and the truth of his principles. A skeleton view of his system might lead you to a cold approbation of his views; but it must be the living, the breathing portraiture of the man that must awaken your love, and dispose you to imitate what you have learned to admire. I have seen him surrounded by his pupils; have marked the overflowings of his tenderness; have read in à thousand traits of good-nature the confirmation of his history. I have witnessed the affecting simplicity with which he speaks of all he has done, and essayed to do, for humanity. Could I convey to others the sentiments I feel for him, he would be loved and honoured as he deserves. Three years of confidential intimacy, every day marked with some proof of his affection, may well have knit my heart to his; and among the most cherished recollections of the past is, that Pestalozzi honoured me with his friendship, and thanked me for cheering his decline. Not that he needs the support of any other mind than his own; his spirit, tender where others suffer, is lofty and self-sustained when affliction assails himself. He, whose house and whose heart were ever the asylum of the distressed, seeks not his own asylum anywhere but in himself. He has tasted the bitterest cup of disappointment, and worn the meanest garb of poverty,—but he broods not over his sorrows ; he weeps for others, and his own heart is relieved : he still hopes for humanity, and his own prospects seem to brighten. Neuhof, the same spot that witnessed his first benevolent exertions, now offers him retirement and repose ; but his heart is still warmed with the longings of his youth, his eye still watches over the progress of his method, and some of his fondest expectations are kindled by our Infant Schools. While he looks back on the labours of his eventful life, he sees failure and disappointment over-throwing every plan in which he has been engaged ; but the same storms that have levelled the parent tree have scattered the seeds of his principles around.*

* The prospect of this often cheered the heart of Pestalozzi amidst privations and trials. In an extract from Dr. Mayo's Introduction to "Lessons on Objects" will be seen the value which he attached to these principles :—" Pestalozzi was peculiarly solicitous that the *idea* of his method of education should not be confounded with the *form* it might assume. He strongly felt the value, the power, and the truth of that *idea ;* and, highly as he was disposed to appreciate the labours of his disciples in the application of it to the work of education, still he saw that they were at best imperfect embodyings of the profound conceptions in which he might be said intellectually

 The subject of this memoir was born at Zurich, in the year 1745. His ancestors were Protestants of Italian extraction, who, during the troubled period of the Reformation, were driven from the Milanese, and had chosen for their abode a city marked for its attachment to their faith. Under its liberal government they had flourished and risen to the first consequence. Pestalozzi's father, however, does not seem to have shared in the general prosperity of the family. His early death left his widow with one son, in very straitened circumstances.*

to live and move. The continual appeal which he made from the imperfections of his practice, to the beauty and truth of his principles, contributed, perhaps, to attach to himself the character of a benevolent visionary, and to his system the charge of impracticability. Much has been written, and much said, yet little seemed to have been done: for even his own school, miserably conducted in many respects, presented but a distorted exhibition of his views. Hence, the man of lofty mind and feeling heart quitted Yverdon with a sigh of regret; while the shallow reasoner and self-satisfied *routier* cast a smile of contempt on principles which he could not discover to be true, in the midst of the disorder that impeded and deformed their development."

* "Pestalozzi's father was an able physician, but ignorant of the arts of life necessary to worldly advancement. Both are attested by the reputation he left behind him, and the mediocrity of his finances. Though reduced to very limited means, the widow was supported in the arduous task which had devolved on her. The advice and interest of the more prosperous branches of the Pestalutz family relieved her desolate condition, and ensured to the growing

·With his dying breath he commended his family to the care of a female domestic; and the fidelity and devotedness with which she discharged the office she undertook impressed on the tender mind of Pestalozzi that strong sense of the virtues of the lower orders, ~that respect and love for the poor which have so marked his character, and exercised so powerful an influence on his life. Barbara sympathized in the family pride, and many were her ingenious contrivances, as Pestalozzi delighted to describe, for maintaining an appearance of respectability in the midst of their poverty. Her great aim seems to have been, to nourish in the mind of her young master that feeling of honest independence which prevailed in those days almost with the intensity of a passion. "Never," she would tell him, "never has a Pestalozzi eaten the bread of private compassion since Zurich was a city. Submit to any privation rather than dishonour your family. Look at those children (she would say as the poor orphans of Zurich passed the windows); how unfortunate would you be were it not for a tender

youth those facilities for entering on an honourable career which, in the small aristocracies of Switzerland, are almost entirely dependent on parentage and connections. A more immediate benefit was derived by Henry from the fostering care of one of those faithful servants of good old patriarchal style, whose character is known in our times as a matter of romance rather than of experience."—*Biber.*

mother, who denies herself every comfort that you may not become a pauper."

If a tinge of haughtiness be sometimes thrown over the dignity of Pestalozzi, to influence like this it might not unreasonably be traced. He himself attributes to it that master passion of his soul, the desire of conferring true independence on the poor, of raising them above the abjectness of poverty, by elevating their characters to endure what they cannot remedy, by developing their faculties that their resources may be increased, and purifying their taste that they may not be wasted.*

Pestalozzi received a tolerable education in a country celebrated for the facility of attaining it.†

*With no companions of his own age, Pestalozzi became so completely a mother's child, that he grew up a stranger to the world he lived in. This lonely childhood had its influence in making him what he remained through life, a man of excitable feelings and lively imagination, which had so entirely the mastery over him as to prevent the exercise of due circumspection and forethought. An anecdote is told which illustrates this trait of character. When, in after years, he was in great pecuniary distress, and his family without the necessaries of life, he went to a friend's house and borrowed a sum of money. On his way home, he fell in with a peasant who was wringing his hands and lamenting the loss of a cow. Carried away, as usual, by his feelings, Pestalozzi gave the man all the money he had borrowed, and ran away to escape his thanks.

† "He was first sent to a day-school, then to a grammar-school, where he was kept under the bondage of rigorous discipline and

Having early abandoned an intention he had formed
of practising the law,* he became deeply interested in

uninteresting tasks, and finally he passed to the college, where he
received due preparation for one of the learned professions, and
thus may be said to have received a good education. His friends
intended that he should become a clergyman, and he had actually
preached a trial sermon, which was a failure, and with his usual
inaccuracy he even went wrong in repeating the Lord's Prayer. Con-
sidering his high moral character, the depth and earnestness of his
piety, his singleness of purpose, and his sympathy with sorrow and
suffering, he seemed pre-eminently calculated for the sacred calling.
When it is considered that Pestalozzi gave, in after life, abundant
proofs of eloquence, it is difficult to attribute to a want of that gift
this change of his career.   It seems more easy to conceive that he,
who was ever ready to raise his voice in defending the oppressed and
pleading for the fatherless, should not feel the same springs of inspiration within him when endeavouring to dash off a probationary
sermon ; and an instinctive perception of the nature of the impedi-
ment might well determine a youth, intimidated by his first failure,
not to expose himself to a second."—*Biber.*

    * Having turned his back on divinity, he applied himself to the
law, impelled, it is said, by his desire of being the champion of the
ill-used peasantry. He regarded legal abuses as the cause of all
their evils, and a righteous law rightly administered as the proper
cure. Consequently, although he had embraced another profession,
the tendency of his mind and views remained the same. Instead
of reading the usual law books, he embarked in speculations on the
best form of government. An essay on the Constitution of Sparta,
and a translation of some of the orations of Demosthenes, which
he published at that period, while they show the turn his studies
had taken, attest his assiduity in research and his proficiency in
classical learning. The further Pestalozzi advanced in his inquiries,

all those schemes for the amelioration of the condition
of the poor, which were at that time agitated in Zurich
by the kind-hearted Lavater, and other friends of
humanity.

His person could never have been very attractive,
and his manners in early life were peculiarly uncouth.
Yet, with these disadvantages, he was happy enough
to form a marriage connection with one of the most
beautiful and amiable women in Zurich, whose faithful
attachment was his support in adversity, and whose
prudence extricated him from a thousand diffi-

and the more he put the existing state of things to the test of those
principles which he had learned to admire, the more was he struck
with the contrast between the professed purpose of society and the
state into which it was actually brought by false and inappropriate
means. He saw that the education of judges and public officers
was not in accordance with the claims of justice and of civil liberty,
nor that of ministers with the spirit of the Gospel ; he saw the worship
of God and the welfare of mankind prostituted to selfish and unholy
purposes ; on the other hand, he saw the people at large unfitted
for the duties of this world, as well as for the claims of the world
to come, by the instruction which they received both at school and
in practical life. The results of his meditations on this subject he
embodied in an essay on the bearing which education ought to have
upon our respective callings, published by him while a student at
law. But Pestalozzi only abandoned the law when he had changed
his views of the means of best benefiting his fellow-countrymen.
Instead of law and politics he embraced philanthropy and education.
He turned his attention to agriculture.

culties.* With the Swiss it is the practice to bury those
relatives to whom they are most tenderly attached in

* The following letter, which he addressed to this lady, gives us
an insight into the noble character as well as the weaknesses of the
writer, and is, moreover, one of the most singular love-letters in
existence :—After telling her that he felt it his duty to limit his visits
to her, as he had not the slightest ability to conceal his feelings, he
proposes a correspondence, in which "we shall make our undis-
guised thoughts known to each other with all the freedom of oral
conversation. I will open myself fully and freely to you ; I will
even now let you look as deep into my heart as I am myself able
to penetrate ; I will show you my views in the light of my present
and future condition as clearly as I see them myself. Dearest
Schultheiss, those of my faults which appear to me most important
in relation to the situation in which I may be placed in after-life are
improvidence, incautiousness, and want of presence of mind to
meet unexpected changes in my prospects. I know not how
far these failings may be diminished by my efforts to counteract
them. At present I have them in such a degree that I dare
not conceal them from the maiden I love ; they are faults,
my dear, which deserve your fullest consideration. I have other
faults, arising from irritability and sensitiveness ; I very frequently
allow myself to run into excesses in praising and blaming, in liking
and disliking ; I cleave so strongly to many things which I possess,
that the force with which I feel myself attached to them often exceeds
the bounds of reason. Whenever my country or my friend is unhappy, I am myself unhappy. Direct your attention to this weakness. There will be times when the cheerfulness and tranquillity of
my soul will suffer under it. Even if it does not hinder me in the
discharge of my duties, yet I shall scarcely ever be great enough to
fulfil them in such adverse circumstances with the cheerfulness and
tranquillity of a wise man who is ever true to himself. Of my very

some favourite part of their garden, that their hours of
retirement may be solemnized by the remembrance of

reprehensible negligence, generally, in all matters which are not in
themselves of importance, I need not speak ; any one may see it at
first sight of me. I also owe you the open confession that I shall
always consider my duties to my beloved partner subordinate to my
duties towards my country ; and that, although I shall be the ten-
derest husband, nevertheless I hold myself bound to be inexorable
to the tears of my wife, if she should ever attempt to restrain me by
them from the direct performance of my duties as a citizen, whatever this must lead to. My wife shall be the confidant of my heart,
the partner of all my most secret counsels. A great and honest
simplicity shall reign in my house. And one thing more. My life
will not pass without important and very critical undertakings. I
shall not forget the precepts of Menalk, and my first resolutions to
devote myself wholly to my country. I shall never, from fear of
man, refrain from speaking when I see that the good of my country
calls upon me to speak. My whole heart is my country's : I will
risk all to alleviate the need and misery of my fellow-countrymen.
What consequences may the undertakings to which I feel myself
urged on draw after them ! How unequal to them am I ! and how
imperative is my duty to show you the possibility of the great
dangers which they may bring upon me !

   " My dear, my beloved friend, I have now spoken candidly of my
character and aspirations. Reflect upon everything. If the traits
which it was my duty to mention diminish your respect for me, you
will esteem my sincerity, and you will not think less highly of me,
that I did not take advantage of your want of acquaintance with my
character for the attainment of my inmost wishes."

   The young lady addressed was worthy of the letter and of its
writer. In 1769, two years after Pestalozzi had established himself
at Neuhof, the marriage took place—an unequal match, as it then

the departed, and their feelings of pleasure still connected with the image of those who were wont to
share them. Two magnificent walnut-trees, in the
garden of the castle of Yverdon, overshadow the simple
grave of Madame Pestalozzi; the children of the poor-
school enriched it with flowers, and Pestalozzi's pensive
moments and fondest recollections were devoted to
the spot.*
It is said that Lavater, foreseeing the influence that
this connection would have on the happiness of his

seemed, the bride having money and personal attractions, and the
bridegroom being notably deficient in both respects. Their married
life extended over fifty years, and during that period the forebodings
of the letter were amply realized. Pestalozzi sacrificed the comfort
and worldly prospects of his family equally with his own to the
public good, and yet we may well believe that Madame Pestalozzi
never repented of her choice.—*Quick.*

* "In December, 1815, Madame Pestalozzi died, aged nearly eighty
years, having been the faithful and patient partner of her husband
during forty-five years of often severe suffering. An incident occurred
at her funeral that showed the strength of Pestalozzi's attachment
to her, his deep trust in God, and the resources he considered the
Bible to possess. After a hymn had been sung, Pestalozzi, turning
toward the coffin, said, "We were shunned and contemned by all, sickness and poverty bowed us down, and we ate dry bread with tears.
What in those days of severe trials gave you and me strength to
persevere, and not to cast away our hope?" Thereupon he took
up a Bible, which was lying near at hand, pressed it on the heart
of the corpse, and said, ' From this source you and I drew courage
and strength and peace.'"—*Von Raumer.*

friend, and on the success of his plans, overcame an attachment he himself had formed for this accomplished woman, and promoted to the utmost of his power the cause of his rival.

Pestalozzi's first enterprise was of an agricultural nature ; * though little prepared by previous education,

* This took place before his marriage, and the history of the transition from law to agriculture is thus told by Dr. Biber:— "Abandoning all his former pursuits, and burning his law papers, he left Zurich and went to Kerchberg, in the canton of Berne, where he apprenticed himself to a farmer of great reputation, not only for his superiority in rural economy, but also for the warm interest he took in the improvement of the agricultural classes. Instead of the lecture-room he frequented the stable ; the sedentary engagements of the study were exchanged for constant exercise in the open air. Occasionally he set his hand to the plough and spade: and whilst he returned to the primitive employment of man, 'to till the ground from whence he is taken,' he was meditating on the best manner of making this simplest of callings the means of mental and moral improvement. The bodily strength which he acquired on this new mode of living braced his weak and irritated nerves ; and his removal from the scene of artificial life enabled him to regain that peace of mind of which his first conflict with the world had deprived him. After he had qualified himself for the conduct of a rural establishment, he employed the small patrimony which his father had left him in the purchase of a tract of waste land in the neighbourhood of Senzburg, in the canton of Berne, on which he erected a dwelling-house with the necessary outbuildings, and gave it the name of Neuhof, that is, New Farm. With all the energy and sanguine anticipations of a young man of twenty-two years, he applied himself to the cultivation of his estate, which, indeed, to

he determined on this career because he conceived that, bringing him into immediate contact with the poor, it might enable him to realize some of his benevolent views in their behalf. At Neuhof he established his first poor-school, the object of which was to show that it was the interest as well as the duty of the proprietors of the soil to bestow the advantages of education on the children of their tenantry. It was a school of industry, as well as of instruction; arranged with a view to develop in the children this sentiment, that *labour was their lot and their duty, their first and most important employment, but that intellectual pursuits were the privilege of their leisure hours.* A cotton manufactory was connected with this scheme, and some part of the instruction was given while the children were actively engaged in it ;*

deserve that name required years of persevering labour. But his courage conquered all difficulties; the work of his hands prospered, and he soon saw his new creation in a flourishing condition, and his prospects as easy and cheerful as he could well have wished."

* Demetz, writing on the agricultural colonies of France, says :—
" It is to the charitable efforts of Pestalozzi that we owe the establishment of agricultural colonies, that is, of institutions, organized on the basis, and in the spirit of the family, with agricultural employment as the principal means of industrial training, and with methods of instruction, moral, intellectual, and physical ; so far as applied, good enough for children of any class of society, and yet capable of being followed by an intelligent mother in the home of the poor. Not that Pestalozzi's own plans and methods, under his own appli-

but Pestalozzi, not having adequate funds, and incapable of attending to those minutiæ on which the success of commercial enterprises in so great a measure depends, soon became embarrassed in his circumstances. But he struggled with ill-fortune, divided his bread with his scholars, and lived himself like a mendicant, that he might teach mendicants to live like men.

After several years of continued labours and privations he was compelled to abandon his enterprise ; but he was never more convinced of the goodness of his project than at the moment when he was obliged

cation, were eminently successful. His institution at Neuhof was a disastrous failure in its immediate results, both as a school and as a pecuniary speculation. ' But the Christian spirit in which this excellent man laboured—the organization into which he gathered the outcasts of society, living among such pupils as a father as well as pastor and teacher, and denying himself the seclusion and comforts of the home which the fortune of his noble-minded wife had secured for him, that he might inspire orphan and even criminal children with filial attachments, cultivate habits of self-reliance and profitable industry, and thus enable them ' to live in the world like men '—this spirit and aim, inaugurated at Neuhof, partially realized at Yverdon, diffused by his writings, and the success of his pupils and disciples in Switzerland and Germany, have led to the establishment of new educational institutions for rich and poor, of schools of practical agriculture, as well as of agricultural reformatories, and at the same time have regenerated the methods of popular education generally."

to renounce it.   In that school of misery the natural kindliness of his character was strengthened into enthusiastic benevolence ; he had drunk deeply of the bitter cup of penury ; but this had quickened his desire to sweeten the draught for others. His intimate connection with the abject poor confirmed his contempt for externals, and his love for unprotected, unportioned humanity.   Above all, the length of his struggle with misfortune had strengthened his constancy and confirmed his reliance on Providence. The habitual disposition of his mind was to appeal from the threatenings of fortune to the mercies of God ; and thus, through the changing tide of chance and pain, he was enabled to hold on his course unfalteringly.   There is a depth in Pestalozzi's sentiments, whether expressed in conversation, portrayed in his writings, or carried out into action, that marks the man who has wrestled with adversity, and knows the bitterest "ills that the flesh is heir to ;" not by report, nor by imagination, but by long and painful experience. This gives to his popular tale, entitled " Leonard and Gertrude," a vigour and freshness of conception, a truth and strength of colouring, which, aided by an original though unpolished style, have made it a lasting favourite with the lower orders in Switzerland. So highly was it esteemed, that many a pastor has assembled his little flock under the village

linden-tree, to read and comment on it for their instruction.*

* " 'Leonard and Gertrude' was written at Neuhof in 1781, and
extorted from him by sympathy with the sufferings of the people.
It was written with a view to deposit in it the knowledge he had
acquired of the condition of the lower classes and the experience he
had gained in attempting their improvement. The vivid colouring
of the picture sufficiently bespeaks his familiarity with scenes of
poverty ; and the warmth of his benevolent sympathy."—*Biber*.

THE FOLLOWING EXTRACTS FROM "LEONARD AND GERTRUDE"
ARE MADE BY DR. MAYO.

" Hubel Rudi was sitting in the midst of his four children. It
was three months since his wife had died, and now his mother lay
on her death-bed. 'Gather up some leaves,' said she, faintly, 'and
put them into my coverlet : I shiver with cold. Oh, Rudi, I am a
sad burthen to you.' 'Dear mother, say not so. You are no
burthen to me. Oh, if I could but afford the help you need ! You
are hungry and thirsty, and utter no complaint : that goes to my
heart, mother.' 'Grieve not, Rudi. When we draw near our end,
we want but little upon earth, and what we want our Father in
heaven sends us. Take comfort, Rudi : I am going to a better
world. You have been the delight of my youth and the consolation
of my old age. All the sorrows of this life tend but to our good.
All the afflictions that I have endured are sanctified to me, and
comfort me more than all the pleasures and enjoyments of life. I
thank God for all the delights of my spring of life, but when in
autumn the fruit ripens and the tree sheds its leaves for the sleep of
winter, then are the trials of life sacred, and its joys but a dream.
I have yet something to tell you, Rudi ; since yesterday it has lain
like a stone upon my heart. I must tell it you. Yesterday I observed
that Rudeli hid himself behind my bed and ate some roasted potatoes
which he took cautiously out of his pocket. Rudi, those potatoes

After some years spent in an obscure retirement,

were not ours. Ah! should this darling child become a thief! How heavily has this thought weighed upon me since yesterday. Where is he? Bring him to me.'

"The child is brought: she raises herself with difficulty, and turning for the last time towards him, takes his two hands between hers, while her feeble, dying head sinks upon his. 'Grandmother,' cried the child, 'what do you want me for? You are not going to die yet; do not die yet, grandmother?' 'Say not so, dear child. I die willingly, since I am going to a beloved Father. Did you but know, Rudeli, with what joy that prospect fills me, you would not thus afflict yourself.' 'Then, grandmother, when you die, I will die with you.' 'No, Rudeli; if it please God, when your father grows old and feeble, then you will be his help and consolation. Surely, Rudeli, you will follow his example. Promise me that, you dear child.' 'Yes, grandmother, indeed I will.' 'Rudeli, our heavenly Father, to whom I am soon going, sees and hears all things; all that we do and all that we promise. Surely, Rudeli, you know that, and you believe it?' 'Yes, grandmother, I know it, and I believe it.' 'Then, why did you come yesterday and eat stolen potatoes behind my bed?' 'Forgive me this time, grandmother.' 'From whom did you steal them?' 'From the mason.' 'You must go to him, Rudeli, and beg him to forgive you. I entreat you, my dear child, though you should be ever so hungry, steal no more. God forsakes no one. Put your trust in a good Providence, and steal no more.' 'Grandmother, indeed I will never steal any more; though I should be ever so hungry, I will never steal any more.' 'Now may the God, in whom is my hope, bless you; may He preserve you, my dear child!'

"The arrival of the bailiffs alarms the dying woman, but she is comforted at hearing that her son is appointed one of the workmen at the church. She then, in a strain of simple piety and homely prudence, gives her last direction to her family. Rudi sets off with

and devoted to the composition of various works,*

the little penitent pilferer to the cottage of Leonard. Pardon is asked, and readily conceded by the kind-hearted Gertrude, who returns with them to the chamber of death. The aged grandmother, assured of her forgiveness, with faltering accents commits the objects of her anxiety to the care of Gertrude, and expires. And thus does human nature ripen for immortality in the dust of the earth.

" Gertrude once more blessed her children, and then returned to her room. Now was she entirely alone; a small lamp glimmered by the side of her, and her heart was solemnly *still*, and her stillness was prayer—silent supplication, a consciousness of the presence and goodness of God, a confident hope of eternal life, and of the happiness in store for them that trust in their Redeemer. Leonard finds her in this state of pious emotion, and regrets that he is not so deeply affected. ' Tears are nothing,' she replies, ' and falling on one's knees is nothing. That one man should be easily excited, and that another should be less so, is of no more consequence than if one stepped lightly, and the other heavily.' "

* The works of Pestalozzi were various, and all were on his darling object—the improvement of the people by means of education. However disappointed he was in the views taken of " Leonard and Gertrude," he would not let the matter end there. He published in the following year his second Book for the People, under the title of " Christopher and Alice." In this work he makes a peasant family read together " Leonard and Gertrude," and say things about the story and the persons introduced into that work, which he thought might not occur to every one. Although it never came into the hands of the lower classes, for whom it was chiefly intended, he hoped to draw the attention of the readers of "Leonard and Gertrude " to the great object of that work, and by familiar illustration of some of the most important topics upon which he had touched, to show how useful lessons might be drawn from a

Pestalozzi was again called into active life.   The

book which was generally considered only in the light of an amusing tale.

The next work of Pestalozzi was of a political character.   Many parts of Switzerland were groaning under vexatious tyranny ; and every attempt on the part of the oppressed to ease their yoke was resisted with the greater obstinacy and violence the more urgently relief was wanted.   Every passion of the human breast was present-ing itself in its most hideous aspect ; and Pestalozzi, who was gifted with penetration into the hidden recesses of the heart, collected the caricatures of human nature, which the time presented to him, in a volume of fables, published under the enigmatic title of " Figures to my Spelling Book."   But this, combined with his well-known political opinions, gained him no friends, while it frustrated his hopes of obtaining assistance from the Swiss Government in carrying on his establishment at Neuhof.   Truly an educator, like a minister of religion, should not be a prominent and one-sided politician ; for education, like Christianity, although the friend and advocate of freedom, is rather personal than political.

The breaking up of the establishment at Neuhof was a fortunate thing for Pestalozzi and for the world.   He was no longer to fritter away his strength in efforts to which he was not equal.   His severe mental and physical labour was not to be in vain ; but was to bear precious fruits.   As the first of these fruits, there appeared in 1780 a paper of his, brief, but full of meaning, in Iselin's Ephemerides, under the title, " The Evening Hour of a Hermit."   It contains a series of concise aphorisms.   They are somewhat metaphysical, and require to be read with attention.   To the thoughtful reader, however, they will be welcome, and they throw light upon Pesta-lozzi's religious opinions, which have been much disputed.   The following are a few selections :—

" What man is, what he needs, what elevates him and degrades him, what strengthens him and weakens him, such is the knowledge

. tempest of the revolutionary war, so afflictive to

needed by the shepherds of the people, and the inmates of the most
lowly hut."

"Everywhere humanity feels this want. Everywhere it struggles
to satisfy it with labour and earnestness. For the want of it men
live restless lives, and at death they cry aloud that they have not ful-
filled the purpose of their being. Their end is not the ripening of
the perfect fruits of the year, which in full completion are laid away
for the repose of the winter."

"Pastors and teachers of the nations know you, man? Is it
with you a matter of conscience to understand his nature, his wants,
his destiny?"

"All mankind are in their nature alike, they have but one path to
contentment and peace."

"The natural faculties of each one are to be perfected into pure
human wisdom. This general education of man must serve as the
foundation to every education of a particular rank."

"Central point of life, individual destiny of man, thou art the
book (aim) of *nature*. In thee lieth the power and the plan of the
wise teacher; and every school education not erected upon the principles of human development leads astray."

"The happy infant learns thus what his mother is to him; and
thus grows within him the sentiment of love and gratitude before he
can understand the words Duty or Thanks."

"The general elevation of these inward powers of the human
mind to a pure human wisdom is the universal purpose of education.
The practice, application, and use of these powers and this wisdom
under special conditions of humanity, is education for a professional
or social condition. These must always be kept subordinate to the
general object of human training."

"The path of nature for developing the faculties of humanity
must be open and easy; and the method for educating man to true
wisdom, simple and universally applicable."

Switzerland, burst with peculiar violence on the

" Nature develops all the human faculties by practice, and their growth depends upon their exercise."

"'The circle of knowledge commences close around a man, and from thence stretches out concentrically."

" Men, fathers, force not the faculties of your children into paths too distant before they have attained strength by exercise in things near them ; avoid harshness and over-fatigue. "

" Real knowledge must take precedence of word-teaching and mere talk."

" All human wisdom is based upon the strength of a good (a sanctified) heart, obedient to truth."

" Knowledge and ambition must be subordinated to inward peace and calm enjoyment."

" As the education for the closest relations precedes the education for more remote ones, so must education in the duties of members of families precede education in the duties of citizens.   But nearer than father or mother is God ; the closest relation of mankind is their relation to Him.   God is also the nearest resource for humanity."

" Faith in God sanctifies and strengthens the tie between parents and children, between servants and masters, between subjects and rulers ; unbelief loosens all ties, annihilates all blessings."

" Sin is the source and consequence of unbelief; it is the transgression of the law, acting contrary to the inward witness of right and wrong, the loss of the childlike mind toward God. "

" Freedom rests upon justice, justice upon love ; therefore freedom also is based upon love.   Justice in families, the purest, most productive of blessings, has love for its source."

" And the source of justice and all blessing for the world, the source of love and brotherly feeling among men, rests on the great thought of religion, that we are children of God (by creation, Acts xvii. ; and to be made children of God in redemption by receiving canton of Unterwalden.   Stanz was consigned to the

Christ, John i. 13) ; and belief of this truth is the sure ground for all blessing for the world."

"The Son of God, the God-Man, who by suffering and death restored (restores) to mankind the universally lost feeling of filial love towards God, is the Redeemer of the world, He is the Sacrificed Priest of the Lord, He is Mediator between God and sinful man. His doctrine is pure justice, teaching educative national philosophy; it is the revelation of God the Father, in His love and mercy, to the lost race of His children."

Much might be said on these aphorisms.   Each is a text for a discourse, and Pestalozzi's life was a paraphrase of these texts.   We must excuse human weakness if the realization of his great antici-pations often turned out miserably, even in glaring contradiction to them.

"On the breaking up of the Neuhof establishment, Pestalozzi, with his family, retired to the Grimsel, and there, in solitude and silence, brooded over the calamities of the fearful times and his own apparent failures.   Of the cause that lay nearest his heart he durst not speak ; a sarcastic hint as to the success of his undertaking would have been the answer.   He was obliged to conceal from mankind the love he bore them, and to take for tender compassion on their part if they considered him no worse than a lunatic.   It was in these calamitous days that Pestalozzi, forgotten by the world, the recollection of which gave him pangs, wrote his ' Inquiries into the Course of Nature in the Development of the Human Species.' This work, published in 1797, marks the transition to a new era in the development of Pestalozzi's views.   Hitherto he had adhered to the outward ; he had mistaken the attendant circumstances of human happiness or misery for their causes.   Neither the partial success which he obtained in his experiment at Neuhof, nor its ultimate failure, were calculated to undeceive him ; for success, which was owing in great measure to a better and holier inflames, and the wretched inhabitants, driven into the

fluence which he exercised over his pupils, was attributed by him
to those outward means which he had employed for the improvement of their condition ; and failure was not so much the effect
of his theoretical mistakes, as the result of a disproportion between
the extent of the undertaking and that of his resources. But when
he saw in the French Revolution all those trammels removed which
he had considered as the causes of human degradation, and found
the emancipated slave, instead of rising in the scale of human
worth, as he had anticipated, on the contrary combining the vices
of his tyrant with those of his former condition ; when he saw
human nature in this pretended self-regeneration more inhuman than
ever; when he saw in his own country the greater number of those
who had been advocates of the rights of mankind trampling those
rights under foot, as soon as the power had passed into their hands,
and substituting the violence of lawlessness and personal despo-
tism to that of misrule and corporate monopoly, then the scales
fell from his eyes. He learned the great truth that in the absence
of external impediments man is even less, than under their pressure,
disposed to seek his own moral and intellectual improvement ; he
saw that there are greater obstacles to be overcome than those
created by the necessities of the earth and the fetters of social life ;
and his mind gradually arrived at the important conclusion that the
amelioration of outward circumstances will be the effect, but never
can be the means, of mental and moral improvement. But when
it is considered how universally it has been the tendency of education to keep the revelations of God distinct as a text-book for a
future existence, and a few scanty fragments of this life that are referred to it, whilst the largest proportion of our present existence is
devoted to objects which have no reference to the other, and made
subject to a rule contrary to that of Christ, it will cease to be a
matter of astonishment that, half a century ago, a Christian in
name, in heart, and in practice was in his philosophy of human life

mountains, suffered the extremes of distress and want.
In the year 1798, Pestalozzi was invited by the
Government to establish a school there,* that the

little better than a Pagan. . . . Let not injustice, therefore,
be done to the memory of a man who was the first to place
mental and moral education upon that basis on which alone it
is possible for it to come under the influence of the power and life of
Christianity. The discovery of that basis had now become the
object of his eager research, and it was not long before he had
an opportunity afforded him of pursuing it on the ground of practical experience, with greater advantage and certainty."—*Biber.*

* The circumstances that led to this invitation are worthy of
record. The bope that the political reform of Switzerland would
of itself produce national improvement was now gone by, and those
who had the welfare of the people at heart began to look out for
some positive influence by which the awakened tendency for new
things might be directed. Switzerland like France was under the
government of a Directory, the most influential member of which
was Legrand, a pure-minded and noble patriot. He was a friend
of Pestalozzi, and had arrived at a decided conviction that national
regeneration, founded upon a better education of all, and especially
of the lower classes, was the only means of turning the late changes
in the social system to some permanently good account. With
Pestalozzi he agreed that to educate men whose happiness should
not depend on their fortunes, nor their virtue on their circumstances
—freemen in the true sense of the word—was the way to save the
cause of liberty from the shipwreck it had suffered in the revolution.
Though tired of the dictatorship, Legrand would not resign until he
had afforded Pestalozzi an opportunity of realizing his views. It
was on the occasion of the Directory distributing favours to their
friends, and asking Pestalozzi what he would have, that he uttered
the noble sentiment which had been formed many years before—" I

children might be rescued from the brutalizing influence of neglect and abject misery. He hesitated
not to accept the proposition. Such was his ardour
to pursue the execution of a plan which had long been
the subject of his thoughts, that neither the most
discouraging circumstances, nor the total want of everything most requisite to its fulfilment, could deter him
from the undertaking.* The children presented

will be a schoolmaster." In order to carry out this resolution he
laid his plans before the Directory. These obtained a most favourable
reception from the Secretaries of State for the Home Department.

The Directory promised to supply him with pecuniary means,
and he was already engaged in selecting an appropriate spot in the
cantons of Zurich and Argovie, when painful events occurred, and
called him to a different sphere of action. The Helvetic Government deeply lamented the sanguinary vengeance with which their
allies had visited one of the States of the ancient Swiss Federation,
and hastened to mitigate the impression which the intelligence of the
event could not fail to produce throughout the land. The most
active measures were taken to rebuild the destroyed dwellings ; the
scattered remnants of the population were invited back under the most
solemn assurances of security, and supplied with provisions. This
was the scene which the Government proposed to Pestalozzi for the
first experiment of his plan of National Education. And Pestalozzi,
regardless of the incalculable difficulties that awaited him, followed
the call of humanity, and, leaving his family behind him, proceeded
to Stanz. He afterwards writes :—"I went: I would have gone
into the remotest clefts of the mountains to come nearer my aim ;
and now I really did come nearer."

* The new convent of the Ursulines, which was in progress of
building, was assigned to him for the formation of an asylum for

themselves in crowds, before there were either chambers, beds, or means for providing for their subsistence. Nearly all, on their arrival, were in a deplorable state, both corporeally and mentally, their appearance bespeaking the most complete degradation of human nature. Some were pale and dejected, the features of each little countenance altered, their looks disturbed, and their foreheads wrinkled with misery and suspicion ; some also were impudent to an excess, full of lies and artifice, corrupted by the habit of begging ; whilst others, bent beneath˙the weight of their afflictions, were patient and docile, but at the same time timid and abashed, and strangers to everything like affection.* A few, whose parents had

orphans and other destitute children ; and ample funds were provided for making the necessary arrangements. But in a country which war had converted into a desert, it was not easy, even with an abundance of pecuniary means, to procure without great delay the most necessary implements for such an establishment. The only apartment habitable on Pestalozzi's arrival was a room of scarcely twenty-four feet square, and this unfurnished.—*Biber.*

* But Pestalozzi's work did not consist merely in reducing such a physical, intellectual, and moral chaos into order, nor did his difficulties arise only from the children and his surroundings. The parents looked upon him as the paid official of a hated Government, distrusted him as a Protestant, annoyed him in every way they could, and encouraged the children in disorder and discontent. Yet the Protestant was giving an example of love and self-sacrifice worthy of the noblest saint in the calendar. This love did not lose its

belonged to the higher classes of society, were spoilt children. Accustomed formerly to all sorts of enjoyment and indulgence, they were full of pretensions and discontent, depressed but not humbled by their misfortunes, envious of each other, and scornful towards their more lowly companions. The only thing which they had in common was the physical, intellectual, and moral neglect to which they had been exposed, and which rendered them all equally fit objects of the most unremitting care, and the most simple and patient instruction.

" My first task," writes Pestalozzi, in a letter to his friend, Gesner, " was to gain the confidence of my pupils, and to attach them to me ; this main point once attained, all the rest appeared to me easy.* Painful as I felt the want of co-operation and assistance, it was precisely what contributed most to the success of

reward. By degrees it gained him the affection of the children, and introduced harmony and order into the class which surrounded him. —*Biber.*

* It has been said that sympathy is the key to a child's heart. Pestalozzi possessed this key, opened the door, entered, and was rewarded with the reciprocated affection of his children. Shakespere (*The Tempest,* Act i. Scene ii.) beautifully represents the power of sympathy over children when he says—

" Thou strokest me, and mad'st much of me.

Would'st teach me how to name the bigger light and how the less,

Which burn by night and day, and then I loved thee."

my enterprise. Cut off from the rest of mankind, I turned all my cares and all my affections to the children.
Whatever relief they received, it was I that administered it ; whatever were their pains or their pleasures,
I was at hand to share them.   I partook of the same
nourishment, and slept in the same chamber; often
from my bed have I given them instruction, or joined
with them in prayer.   When they were well, I was
everywhere with them ; and when they were sick, I
was still at their bedside."*

"In 1799," continues Pestalozzi, "my school contained nearly eighty pupils, the greater part of whom
announced good dispositions, and some even first-rate
abilities.   Study was to them quite a novelty, and
they attached themselves to it with indefatigable zeal
as soon as they began to perceive their own progress.†

* The language of a master of one of our English Reformatory
Schools is almost as sublime.   "You see, my work here is not easy,
for I have to be father and mother, brother and sister, all in one, to
these boys—father to enforce law sternly and inflexibly, yet lovingly
too—mother to represent the Divine tenderness, and gentleness, and
compassion—brother and sister to be their sympathizing playmates."
—A Sermon by the Hon. and Rev. W. H. Lyttelton, on the Original
Order of Nature our Model, and the Spirit of God our Guide, in the
Work of Education.

† "The great stimulus to labour," says Currie, "is the hope of
success ; without this motive the children are so weak that they will
not readily feel its force of themselves, they will not even make the
attempt, but assume its impossibility.   The prestige of success has

The very children who had never had a book in their hands before, applied themselves from morning till night ; and when I have asked them, after supper, ' My children, which would you rather do—go to bed, or learn a little longer?' they would generally reply that they would rather learn. The impulse was given, and their development began to take place with a rapidity that surpassed my most sanguine hopes. In a short time were seen above seventy children, taken almost all from a state of poverty, living together in peace and friendship, full of affection for one another, and with a cordiality that rarely exists among brothers and sisters in large families. I had never given them as

a mighty influence on the pupil. What he has been shown he can do he will willingly try again ; ' no one hates what he can do tolerably well, even though it be dry and uninteresting' in itself ; there is a feeling of self-gratulation which disposes to a repetition of the effort ; whereas, the conviction that it is of no use to try is a kind of mental paralysis from which it is the first and last object of good teaching to save the child." Akin to this is the pleasure of success, in which hope is changed into fruition. It is one of the strongest principles of human nature, and teachers should not be slow to avail themselves of it. However slow and unwilling at first, let the minds of children be set in motion, and the impetus will carry them forward. Success in learning is like the acquisition of money, the more is gained the greater the desire to acquire. The teacher, however, must not trust to its spontaneous operation, but encourage its exercise by sympathy and congratulation. Thus whilst influenced by the teacher he would be learning to depend upon himself with increasing trust in his own power.

yet direct lessons, either in religion or morality; but when they were assembled around me, and when there was a dead silence among them, I said to them, 'When you behave thus, are you not more reasonable beings than when you make a riot?' And when they used to embrace me, and call me their father, I would say, 'Yes, you are ready to call me father, and yet you do behind my back things which disoblige me; is this right?'* Sometimes I would set before them

---

* In matters of domestic discipline he endeavoured, by an appeal to their feelings and good sense, to give them such a view of the nature of the case as would induce them to impose on themselves those restrictions which were absolutely necessary. If some disorder arose from inattention to little things, he would say to them, "You see, now, how this great disorder has come upon us by a trifling neglect. Does not this show that in so large a household every little matter should be carefully attended to?" At other times, if it became necessary to correct a child of some bad habit, he would tell him, "It is not on your account only that I must desire you to leave off this practice, but on account of the other boys also, who might learn it from you, and so might acquire a habit which it would be difficult for them to conquer. And do you not think that you yourself would not get rid of it easily if you saw others doing the same thing, so that you would be constantly tempted by their example?" Not only did he gain his point in almost every case, but he awakened in his pupils a general interest in the maintenance of good order, which proved far more efficient than any rules and penal inflictions by which a slavish conformity is commonly enforced. Of this training character was the following incident:— On one occasion, when some of the inhabitants of the Grisons, whom war and political persecution had driven from their homes, passed

the picture of a peaceable and orderly family, who, having acquired easy circumstances by their labour and economy, found themselves capable of giving advice and assistance to their ignorant, unfortunate, and indigent fellow-creatures ; then addressing myself to those in whom I had perceived the most lively disposition to benevolence, I would say, ' Should you not like to live as I do, in the midst of the unfortunate, to direct them, and to make them useful to themselves and to society ? ' Then, with tears in their eyes, and with the generous glow of sensibility on their little countenances, they would reply, ' Oh ! yes, could we but hope to accomplish it.' * When Altorf was

through Stanz, and having visited his establishment, presented him with a small sum of money for his children, he called them together, and said, " These men, you see, have been obliged to flee from their homes, so that they know not where they shall lay their heads to-morrow ; and yet, in their own distress, they have made you this present ; so I thought you would like to come and thank them your-selves." The scene which ensued was so affecting that the strangers took their leave with tears in their eyes.—*Biber*.

* This was moral teaching by sympathy, precept, and example ; but Pestalozzi was not satisfied with this. " With him teaching was not so much to be thought of as training. Training must be found for the child's heart, head, and hand, and the capacities of the heart and head must be developed by practice no less than those of the hand. Pestalozzi would have the charities of the family circle intro-duced into the schoolroom, and would have the child taught virtue by his affections being exercised, and his benevolence guided to action." " Training " and the " Training System " have generally

reduced to ashes, I assembled them around me.
'Altorf,' said I, 'is destroyed; and at this moment,
perhaps, there are more than a hundred poor
children without clothes to cover them, without a
house, or a morsel of bread to eat. Shall we petition
the Government to permit us to receive twenty of
them amongst us?' Methinks I still see the eagerness
with which they replied, 'Yes! oh, certainly! yes!'
'But, consider well,' replied I, 'what you are about
to ask; we have at present but very little money at
our command, and it is doubtful whether they will
grant us any more in favour of these unfortunates.
Perhaps, in order to maintain your existence and carry
on your instruction, it will be necessary to labour
much more than you have ever yet done; perhaps it
may be necessary to divide with these strangers your
victuals and your clothes; do not say, then, you will
receive them among you if you are not sure you will
be able to impose upon yourselves all these privations.'
I gave to my objections all the force they were
capable of; I repeated to them all I had said, to be
sure that they perfectly understood me; still they persevered in their first resolution—'Let them come,'

been traced to a nearer source and later period; but Pestalozzi
practised and taught the doctrine of intellectual development and
moral training long ere Mr. Stowe, the benevolent Scotchman, had
an educational existence.

said they, 'let them come ; let all you have said prove true, we will divide with them what we have.'"

Destitute of those aids to intellectual instruction which schools usually possess, without assistants, and with few books, Pestalozzi found himself involved in difficulties sufficient to have overwhelmed a man of ordinary talents ; but they served only to develop *his* resources, and to open a path for the march of *his* genius. He did not, indeed, enjoy the facilities of a regular establishment, but he was unencumbered by its trammels and unfettered by its routine. Nature became the school-book ; and in the actual experience and self-acquired knowledge of his pupils, he found those elements of instruction which are usually sought in the discoveries of other minds and the abstractions of science.* His scholars might be acquiring little of what is generally called *learning*, but the activity and vigour of their minds, the clearness and precision of their ideas, convinced Pestalozzi that *life not only presents the best opportunities for moral culture,*† *but*

---

* See "Pestalozzi and his Principles," the second part of this work.

† In this memoir there have been given several instances of life being used as opportunity for moral culture. The following are added because of the importance of the principle and its superiority over any system of training by means of lessons which are outside the sphere of experience, or of injunctions that are either negative in their character or abstract in their nature, and consequently irksome

*furnishes also the most valuable materials for intellectual development.**

Pestalozzi accustomed his pupils to make observations on the objects that surrounded them, and to express with accuracy the ideas which they thus acquired. Their entire ignorance led him to rest long on the elements of every branch of instruction he was enabled to introduce, and he saw the beneficial consequences of rendering perfect their knowledge of the first steps, in the firmness which it

and reluctantly obeyed. The Incidental Lessons that were formerly given in Infant Schools approximated to this teaching of Pestalozzi ; but with the introduction of stereotyped courses of lessons which often have no application to the circumstances and wants of the children, and time-tables which must be fixed for the year—this good practice has fallen into some disuse. There is a tendency in the anticipation and preparation of lessons to make work occupy a more prominent place than want — the teacher and inspector to have a prior claim to the child. Not so with Pestalozzi, and it ought not to be so with those who profess to have learned from his disciples.

* Life furnishes materials for intellectual development. "Not one of the little incidents in the life of a child, in his amusements and recreations, in his relation to his parents and friends and play-fellows, nor anything within reach of a child's attention, but may be made the object of a lesson by which some useful knowledge may be imparted, and by which the child may be familiarized with the habit of thinking on what he sees, and speaking after he has thought. The mode of doing this is not to talk much to a child, but to enter into conversation with him ; to bring him to express

gave their minds, and in the consciousness of power
which it inspired.*

The number of his pupils led him to adopt the
principle of *mutual instruction*—one of those simple
means which nature offers, and which good sense,
quickened by necessity, has applied in every country

himself on the subject ; not to exhaust the subject, but to question
the child about it, and to let him find out and correct the answers.
It would be ridiculous to expect that the volatile spirits of a child
could be brought to follow any lengthy explanations. The attention
is deadened by long expositions, but roused by animated questions,
which should be short, clear, and intelligible, exciting him to observe,
to recollect, to compare, and to muster his little stock of
knowledge for materials for an answer."—*Biber*. When an object
has been submitted to the senses of a child, he must be led to the
consciousness of the impressions produced, and then must be
taught the name of the object and of the qualities producing
those impressions. Last of all, he must ascend to the definition
of the object.

* In his letters to Greaves, Pestalozzi says : — " Their total
ignorance forced me to dwell a long time on the simplest elements,
and I was led to perceive how much higher a degree of interest is
obtained by persevering attention to the elementary parts until they
be perfectly familiar to the mind ; and what confidence the child is
inspired with by the consciousness of complete attainment, even in
the lowest stage of instruction. Never before had I so deeply felt
the important bearing which the first elements of every branch of
knowledge have upon its complete outline, and what deficiencies in
the final result must arise from the confusion and imperfection of
the simplest beginnings. To bring these to maturity in the child's
mind became now a main object of my attention ; and the success

and in every age. Mutual instruction, however, in his hands, was an engine very different from the machinery of the Madras system. *It was founded on the simple relations and affectionate feelings of domestic life, not on the principles of political institutions and the duties of civil subordination.**

He had already endeavoured to connect the education of the pupil with the experience of the child ; he now wished to unite the labours of the pupil with the business of the adult. With him the genius of education took the form of the

far surpassed my expectations. The consciousness of energies hitherto unknown to themselves was rapidly developed in the children, and a general sense of order and harmony began to prevail among them. They felt their own powers, and tediousness vanished like a spectre from the room. They were determined to try, and succeeded ; they persevered, they accomplished, and were delighted. Their mood was not that of laborious learning, it was the joy of unknown powers aroused from sleep ; their hearts and minds were elevated by the anticipation of what their powers would enable them to attempt and to effect."

* The adoption of the monitorial system in his school was one application of a principle which contemplated moral training as a primary consideration and mutual instruction as subsidiary to it. Dr. Biber tells us that " the design of making all the children under his care view each other in the light of brethren led him to render them, in a variety of ways, dependent upon each other. Each child, according to his age and abilities, was in his turn engaged in employments, of which the others were to reap the benefit ; and as their mutual services were not compulsory, they were kindly proffered and thank-

fabled Janus—one face looking to the past of

fully received. The advantage of this arrangement became particularly visible in school hours, when the more advanced boys acted as assistant teachers, by which means the task of furnishing so large a number of children, differing widely in ages, in natural capacities, and acquirements, with occupation adequate to the peculiar wants of each individual was greatly facilitated. But powerful as the aid was which Pestalozzi derived from this plan for the communication of knowledge, this was by no means its primary object or its most beneficial result. The promotion of mutual kindness was to him more important than the carrying on of mutual instruction ; and hence the latter had in his school not a dead mechanism, devised for the purpose of propelling the children in the course of a certain routine, and kept alive by selfish motives ; but it had the spontaneous effect of the common tie of love, inducing them to assist each other in the acquisition of knowledge : children became the teachers of children. " They endeavoured to carry into effect what I proposed, and in doing so, they themselves frequently traced the means of execution. Their spontaneous activity was called out in every direction, as far as the elements of knowledge went ; and I was brought to the firm conviction that all instruction, to have a truly enlightening and cultivating influence, must be drawn out of the children, and, as it were, be begotten within their minds." "To this," says Pestalozzi, "I was brought chiefly by necessity. Seeing that I had no assistant teacher, I placed a child of superior capacities between two of inferior powers. He threw his arms round their necks ; he taught them what they knew ; and they learned from him what they knew not. They sat by the side of each other with heartfelt affection. Joy and love animated their souls ; the life which was awakened within them carried both teachers and learners forward with a rapidity and cheerfulness which this process of mutual enlivening alone could produce."

But the mutual instruction of Pestalozzi is nct to be confounded life, and the other to the future.* He had just

with the monitorial system of Bell and Lancaster. Pestalozzi employed one child to teach another : this is mutual instruction ; Bell
and Lancaster employed one child to teach another: this too is
mutual instruction. But Pestalozzi awakened in one child a consciousness of his powers and a tendency to mental self-activity ;
and the child so awakened he called in to assist him in awakening
other children in the same manner by the same means. Pestalozzi
led his children by the moral ascendancy which he had gained over
them ; so that whithersoever he led the way, they were willing to
follow ; and in the same manner he taught his children to treat one
another. Bell and Lancaster, on the contrary, drilled one child
through an artificial machinery of lifeless tasks ; and the child so
drilled they employed to drill others in the same manner, and by the
same means. Bell and Lancaster restrained their children by fear,
and excited them by artificial and mercenary motives, that the
natures of the children might yield to the *unnature* of the system ;
and the same means of direct and indirect compulsion they placed
in the hands of their subordinate drillers."

*This is the true theory of education, both in its instructional
and disciplinary departments, but one that I fear is often neither
known nor felt. It is this that so completely separates the Infant
School from the Elementary, and even the Junior from the Senior
departments of the latter. The infant lives in the present ; it is hard
to get him to look forward. Well is it that it is so. To be engaged
with his present and past experience alone is nature's method of
affording him means of growth and happiness, physical, intellectual,
and moral. At least in the teaching department the wants, capabilities, and methods of dealing with infants were not practically
recognized till the establishment of the Home and Colonial School
Society. A glance at the subjects and methods of instruction given
in the Manuals of that Society will show the difference between the
Infant and Juvenile Schools in this respect.

succeeded in introducing some manual employment into his school when the thread of his labour was rudely snapped by political changes, and, exhausted in mind and body, assailed by ridicule, and depressed by disappointment, he sought to recruit his powers by retirement and relaxation.*

Pestalozzi had gained much experience at Stanz ; and when, under the patronage of the Swiss Government, he resumed his labours at Burgdorf, in the Canton of Berne, he brought his first vague, but powerful impressions to the form of clear and distinct ideas : he settled the main features of his system of education.† At Burgdorf he was joined by several men of various degrees of talent and

---

* In little more than a year after he settled at Stanz, sickness broke out among the children, and the wear and tear were too great even for Pestalozzi. He would probably have sunk under his efforts, if the French, pressed by the Austrians, had not entered Stanz in January, 1799, and taken part of the Ursuline Convent for a military hospital. Pestalozzi was, therefore, obliged to break up the school, and he himself went to a medicinal spring on the Gurnigel, in the Canton of Berne. " Here," he says, " I enjoyed days of recreation. I needed them. It is a wonder that I am still alive. I shall not forget those days as long as I live. They saved me ; but I could not live without my work." He accordingly left his retreat, and once more entered the field of labour in the town of Burgdorf, in the Canton of Berne.

† For an account of his first efforts at Burgdorf, see " Pestalozzi and his Principles."

attainment. The enthusiasm of his character kindled
all the energies of theirs ; and the bold suggestions
of his genius, though at first imperfectly understood
or unwillingly admitted, ripened in their minds to
connected plans of elementary education. He taught
them that reading, writing, and arithmetic were
not the real elements of instruction, * but that a
simpler, a more natural foundation must be sought.
The basis of all sound knowledge, argued he, is the
accurate observation of things acting on the outward senses.† Unless physical conceptions be formed

* One only wonders that reading, writing, and arithmetic could ever
have been regarded as the foundations or elements of knowledge.
It is now generally understood that they are not knowledge, but
mere instruments of knowledge, most useful in the intercourse and
business of life. It is to be feared that with many teachers their
relation to knowledge is not sufficiently felt and applied, by the
child being led to take an interest in the acquisition of the instrument for the sake of the knowledge which it obtains. It is in this
way that teachers fail to employ one of the most powerful motives
to interest in learning to read, write, and cypher. I often admire
the tact of our present mistress of the Model Infant School, who
appoints regular periods for reading interesting stories, etc., to her
younger children, and furnishing her elder with simple, interesting,
and illustrated children's books from the school library. The meagre
explanations of the reading-lesson, and the absence of a school
library in many of our schools, prove how little is understood the
relation of the instrument to the work it is designed to accomplish.

† In the Preface to the 14th Edition of her "Lessons on
Objects," written in 1855, Miss Mayo remarks :—"When this work

with distinctness, our abstractions will be vague
and our judgments and reasonings unstable.* *The*
was first presented to the public, nearly thirty years since, the idea
of systematically using the material world as one of the means of
educating the minds of children was so novel a thing in England,
that the title of ' Lessons on Objects ' excited many a smile, and the
success of the little volume was deemed to be, at best, very dubious.
The sound sense of the plan, however, soon recommended it to our
teachers, and they discovered that reading, writing, and arithmetic
do not form the sole basis of elementary education, but that the
objects and actions of every-day life should have a very prominent
place in their programme. In spite of the forebodings which
attended the first introduction of this little volume, the public has given
a decided sanction to the system of teaching it, and the degree in
which it has in consequence modified books for the young, and the
practice of elementary instruction, can scarcely be calculated."

'' In Lessons on Objects, in which were laid the foundations of
knowledge, Pestalozzi had a threefold aim. 1. Enlarging the
sphere of a child's observation by increasing the number of objects
falling under his immediate perception. 2. Impressing upon him
those perceptions of which he had become conscious, with clearness,
depth, and precision. 3. Imparting to him a comprehensive knowledge of language for whatever had become an object of his consciousness. In the course of such instruction the pupil is often
required to recollect what he has learnt, and to institute comparisons
in which he discovers both resemblances and differences. From
observation and memory there is only one step to reflection.
Though imperfect, this operation is often found among the early
exercises of the infant mind. The powerful stimulus of inquisitive-
ness prompts to exertion, which, if encouraged, will lead to a habit
of thought."—*Letters to Greaves.*

* The influence of observation goes beyond the fact of its being
the ground of real knowledge, and this should form an irresistible

first object, then, in education, must be to lead a child to observe with accuracy; the second, to express with correctness the result of his observations. The practice of embodying in language the conceptions we form, gives permanence to the impressions; and the habit of expressing ourselves with the utmost precision of which we are capable, mainly assists the faculty of thinking with accuracy and remembering with fidelity.*

argument for the cultivation of the senses in childhood. Cultivated perception excites attention, and brings it into activity; it is necessary to clearness and richness of conception, and even plays the part of handmaiden to imagination, whilst it contributes to render clearer general ideas, and to create associations intended to influence the character. Moreover, Nature calls for the cultivation of the senses as the first work to be done in education. From surrounding objects are heard ten thousand sounds, and the ear is acted on; light is reflected from numerous bodies, strikes on the eye, and vision takes place; the air is impregnated with various perfumes, and the sense of smell takes cognizance of their presence and qualities. Within the child, in the constant desire to exercise the senses, Nature utters an equally loud voice. We know that when unrestrained the infant acts from an early period in almost instinctive obedience to the external call of Nature: it delights to exercise its eye on brilliant objects and colours, its ear in the discrimination of sounds by every variety of noise, and to educate the sense of touch by feeling and handling everything within its reach.

* We have here two important thoughts respecting the position of language in education: first, in relation to ideas; second, its influence in the cultivation of the mind. The school of Pestalozzi

Never were Pestalozzi's hopes, full as he always had been of that element of genius, raised to a higher pitch than at Burgdorf. Scholars of every age and of almost every rank flocked to his establishment : his coadjutors, animated by the same spirit, laboured incessantly to advance and apply his theory, and to execute it with fidelity in the class-room. Men of property and talent watched his movements with interest, eager to avail themselves of his plans for the moral and intellectual improvement of the lower orders. Meanwhile, the patronage of the Swiss Government augmented his pecuniary resources, and furnished him with a suitable field for his exertions. But political changes again broke up, like an ant's nest, the rising institution.*

has never ignored language, whether for its instructional or educative power. It has clearly defined its function, marked its place, and pointed out its use. What Dr. Mayo means by expressing "the result of observation" is, that, as a rule, the young child ought not to have a term given him until he feels the need of it, or has grasped the idea of the thing signified. This takes place when the idea has been formed in his mind, and then he will not only be able to use it, but feel pleasure in doing so. This method forms a prominent feature in infant teaching ; good teachers at the reading-lesson often give the subject first orally, that they may introduce ideas and words in their right order ; they are careful that the language of the piece shall not be merely explained by simple words, but by illustrations addressed to the senses.

* On the restoration of the Cantons in 1804, the Castle of Burgdorf was again occupied by one of the chief magistrates, and

The next period of Pestalozzi's career commences with the formation of two separate establishments, consisting, for the most part, of his former pupils. The children of the poorer class took up their abode at Munchen Buchsee, a little village within a mile of Hofwyl, and about five miles from Berne. Here he was much aided by M. de Fellenberg, who . has since applied his principles of education, with some important modifications, to the instruction of both rich and poor. Whilst at Yverdon, in the Canton de Vaud, he resumed his labours for the instruction of the higher and middle ranks of society.*

Pestalozzi and his establishment were moved to the monastery of Buchsee.

* On receiving notice to quit Burgdorf by the magistrates of the Canton of Berne, Pestalozzi was invited by Emmanuel de Fellenberg, who proposed that the whole institution should be removed to his estate at Buchsee. Although De Fellenberg was celebrated as a patron of education, possessed of pecuniary means and distinguished for all the personal qualities requisite for the administration of an extensive undertaking, yet Pestalozzi would not accept the offer. " He dreaded the danger of marring the internal success of his institution by subjecting it to the influence of views which bore no analogy whatever to his own. Fellenberg was endeavouring to trace out the most efficient way for rendering his pupils fit members of society; his education was essentially an education for the world; every child was placed in his establishment in that rank in which he would have to appear hereafter in life; his occupations, instruction, mode of living were all calculated to prepare him for his social position.

The fame of his method was now very generally spread through Switzerland and Germany, and young men from all quarters assembled under his paternal roof to act as instructors.' Pupils from

Pestalozzi's object, on the contrary, was by the most direct, though it might be the slowest course, to foster the internal growth of the intellectual and moral man; to the claims of the world he turned a deaf ear; he asked not for what society, but for what God, had destined the child; his education was essentially in reference to the purpose of God, and the position of each pupil in his establishment was accordingly founded, not upon the artificial institutions of society, but upon a spirit of freedom and brotherly love."—*Biber.* It is much to be regretted that Pestalozzi did not close with the offer of De Fellenberg; there was so little difference in their views of the function of education, and none in their conviction that education alone was the means of blessing their country. The distinction drawn between their views by Dr. Biber is one of difference of standpoint, and a difference not only easily reconcilable, but necessary to completeness. To make education complete, the threefold relation of the child must be regarded: the *personal*, in which all his faculties should be brought to the highest perfection of which they are capable, and thus be made a *man;* the *social*, in which he ought to be prepared for the right discharge of the duties of life, and thus be made a *citizen;* and the *religious*, in which he is connected with God, and requires to know His name, character, and grace with respect to himself—the claims He has upon him and the duties he owes—and thus become a *Christian.* Pestalozzi simply appeared to lay most stress on the first relation, and De Fellenberg on the second. Whilst we know that Pestalozzi would prepare for life, whilst De Fellenberg educated the faculties, one cannot but feel that the idiosyncrasies of the men were stamped on their peculiarities—the one being a Liberal aristocrat, and the other a thorough-going Radical,

E

every part of Europe constituted one happy family around him. They formed numerous classes, each having at its head an instructor, who lived with his scholars, directing their studies and sharing their amusements; and while he thus connected himself with their pleasures as well as their duties, was enabled to win their affections and gently mould them to his purpose. The virtues of Pestalozzi were the bond that united them. His simple piety taught them to regard the Almighty as their common Father in whose continual presence they lived.

with something bordering on Communistic principles, only controlled by benevolence and conscience. In this country we should naturally sympathize with De Fellenberg regarding the gradations of society as both necessary and beneficial, whilst they are united by mutual service, to which are added benefits conferred by one and received by the other. There is also some slight suspicion of lower motives being at work in the refusal. When the institution was removed from Burgdorf to the monastery of Buchsee, the teachers voted De Fellenberg to the direction, which, Pestalozzi himself tells us, was not only without his consent, but to his profound mortification. This is the only case in which Pestalozzi yielded to anything but a self-sacrificing devotedness to the promotion of popular education. It may be that the two distinguished men effected more for education apart than they would have done together. At all events, soon after the above occurrence, Pestalozzi accepted an invitation from the inhabitants of Yverdon to open an institution there, and within a twelvemonth he was followed by his old assistants, who had found government by Fellenberg less to their taste than government by Pestalozzi.

and on whose constant bounty they had to rely.
They were led to regard one another as brethren;
and the affection with which their masters treated
them, and which overflowed in every word and
action of Pestalozzi himself, contributed to impart a
character of mutual kindness and love to the whole
group. His religious influence was limited to the
cultivation of pious feelings ; the formation of their
opinions, the inculcation of their particular mode
of faith, was left to the ministers, or teachers, of
their respective persuasions.*

The Yverdon Institution has proved the fruitful
source from which many establishments have emanated ; in some of which the views of Pestalozzi
are closely followed, while in others they are materially modified, or admitted only in particular
branches.† His own Institution, undermined by ill-

---

* Dr. Biber gives us a picture of the Yverdon Instituticn, which
shows more fully the influence of the patriarchal government of
Pestalozzi. (See second part of this work.)

† Dr. Mayo, writing long before Training Colleges were established, utters the following admirable sentiment on the subject
which was practically though not systematically carried out at
Yverdon :—" Whenever," says Dr. Mayo, "improved principles of
popular education are advocated, this difficulty is invariably started,
'where shall we find persons competent to execute these views?'
Men must be trained, they must be taught to teach, educated to
educate. We have had enough of books adapted to disguise the

regulated generosity and want of order, has been
finally ruined by disagreement among his coadjutors,
by mismanagement of his pecuniary resources, and
by confidence ill-placed and ill-requited.* After a

ignorance of the teacher and perpetuate that of the pupil ; we must
now form *men ;* we must bring the living mind in contact with
mind, the living heart in contact with the heart. Whenever the
Government of the country shall be fully persuaded that an *improved*
as well as extended system of education is the greatest boon it can
bestow on the people, schools for teachers will doubtless be formed.
On the wisdom that presides over their formation, on the moral and
religious spirit that pervades their operations, will mainly depend
the character of the rising generation. Happy will it be for us, if
taught at last by painful experience we seek to diffuse moral discipline and religious influence through all our national institutions
for education. A more intelligent population we may expect to find,
when the teacher shall feel it a more important work to cultivate
reflection and judgment than to load the memory with ill-digested
knowledge. A better and a happier generation we may hope, under
the Divine blessing, to see, when the educator, whatever rank he
may hold, whether instructing our young nobility, training up the
children of the middle classes, or labouring in a poor-school, shall
feel that he is abandoning the most important post, and compro-
mising his most sacred duty, when he neglects to form the moral
character of his pupils on the basis of religious principle. ' L'édu-
cation sans réligion n'est que le vernis.' Alas for the times in which
loud-mouthed efforts are being made for divorcing religion from our
schools, and a gradual and practical rejection of the possession of
religion by our school teachers ! "

* " The Yverdon Institution was of world-wide reputation.
Pestalozzian teachers went from it to Madrid, to Naples, to St.
Petersburg. Kings and philosophers joined in doing it honour.

long series of vexations and disappointments, he
has been driven into an involuntary retirement, and
the clouds which alternately darkened the prospects
of earlier years, and were dispersed by his energy
and talent, seem settling over the sunset of his days.

At how dear a rate, with how great a sacrifice
of private interest and personal comfort, is pur-
chased the glorious privilege of essentially benefiting
humanity ! The gifted individual who conveys to
his fellow-mortals the torch of truth is worn out
by the intensity of his feelings ; and his spirit,
though often restored by hope, is at last consumed
by continual disappointment. Such has been the
destiny of Pestalozzi : yet now, at the close of life's
career, he looks back on the painful journey he has
trodden, and is enabled to trace in many of the difficulties of his prime of life a discipline necessary for
the attainment of that practical success which par-

But as Pestalozzi himself has testified, these praises were but as a
laurel wreath encircling a skull. The life of the Pestalozzian
institutions had been the love which the old man had infused into
all the members, teachers as well as children ; but this life was
wanting at Yverdon. The establishment was much too large to be
carried on successfully without more method and discipline than
Pestalozzi, remarkable, as he himself says, for his ' unrivalled
incapacity to govern,' was master of. The assistants began each to
take his own line, and even the outward show of unity was soon at
an end."—*Quick.*

tially, at least, has adorned his decline. He looks not to his own life for the winding-up of the drama : he casts his eye forward into a long futurity, and enjoys the cheering anticipation that a few scenes of sorrow will lead to the happiest results. Had his advantages been greater, he concludes that his success would have been easier, but less complete. The practical application of his views would sooner have been made, but his principles would have been less profound.

The frequency of Pestalozzi's failures has been unfairly urged as presumptive evidence against the truth and practicability of his views; but it must be remembered that political events, over which he could exercise no control, occasionally involved him in ruin ; and, on the other hand, to what can we attribute the frequent revival of his system, unfavoured as the founder was with the gifts of fortune, but to the elastic, the imperishable nature of that truth on which it is built ? The imperfections of his character may have contributed to overthrow the fabric of his institutions, but the foundation of his principles remains uninjured ; and the errors and misfortunes of the master form a beacon for the guidance and warning of his disciples.*

* The imperfections of Pestalozzi's character were eminently calculated to overthrow all his efforts towards the organization of his

The religious opinions attributed to Pestalozzi have prejudiced many against his method. But though some errors have deformed his creed, and much vagueness and uncertainty hung over his mind, yet as these belong to his individual character, and are unconnected with the practical application of his principles of education, it would be the height of injustice to attribute them, without further evidence, to any one who professes to admire or act upon his system. Filial respect and attachment will dictate the course which his disciples will pursue. They will drop the mantle of charity over his weakness and errors, while they gratefully acknowledge that it is to his genius they are indebted

system. Whenever he had to manage men and things, his imprudence involved him in many a difficulty ; whilst his want of tact was an obstacle to dealing with persons and applying his own principles. The rapidity with which ideas flowed upon him left but little time for testing and application. It is to be deeply regretted that Pestalozzi did not know wherein his great strength lay, and wherein his weakness. Had he come into as close contact with De Fellenberg as he did with Fisher, the Home Secretary of the Directory, he might have been as successful in inspiring him with reverence for his unrivalled genius and the soundness of his principles. De Fellenberg would have supplied all Pestalozzi's deficiences, and even improved his system, in converting the ideal into the real, and bringing it into conformity with practical life. The deficiencies of Pestalozzi were few, but fundamental, and they are pointed out as a warning to those who in the best spirit and with the noblest motives might repeat the same mistakes.

for those principles of education which they labour to unfold and apply.*

* That the religious opinions of Pestalozzi had nothing to do with his principles and his system of education, is proved by the fact that the large and important school for the sons of the nobility and gentry at Cheam, which Dr. Mayo established and conducted ; and the Home and Colonial School Society founded by John Stuckey Reynolds, John Bridges, and others, for the application of his principles among the poor, have both been conducted on sound evangelical principles, the pupils receiving a religious education in accordance with the doctrinal Articles of the Church of England. Pestalozzi's religious views were on most great and fundamental points accurate. The man who used the following language must have been on a par with the majority of religious men. " There is none other name, dear child. The name of Jesus Christ is Jesus Christ Himself in the entire perfection of His Godhead and Manhood. Never name the name of Christ without calling to mind the words of Moses, ' Thou shalt not take the name of the Lord thy God in vain.' " The man who admitted the Deity of our Lord, and, as seen in his aphorisms of the " Evening Hours of a Hermit," the sacrificial character of our Lord's work, must have held collateral truths of the Gospel, and could not have been lost amidst the mists of German Rationalism. The piety of Pestalozzi was deep and fervent, that breathing, active piety that would throw life into our clearer, but, alas! often colder views of Gospel truth. Whilst we talk about the Gospel and expound its doctrines, exhibiting our regard for its truths, Pestalozzi would *feel* and *act*, and thus give a practical illustration of the temper and spirit of the Gospel. This characteristic of Pestalozzi's piety had its influence in the formation of his system of education. It led him to conclude that a moral and religious education is not so much to be conducted by precept as by fact, by feeling and by conduct. It was probably this also which led him to estimate at a comparatively low rate the

Dr. Mayo concludes this memoir with a summary of the principles of Pestalozzi, which will be found in the second part of this work. And in a note, in melancholy and touching tones, he remarks, "Pestalozzi is no more. After a short but painful illness, he died near Neuhof, in the Canton of Argau, in the month of February, 1827." "The sun went down in clouds, and the old man, when he died at the age of eighty, had seen the apparent failures of all his toil. He had not, however, failed in reality. It has been said of him that his true function was to educate ideas, not children ; and when, twenty years later, the centenary of his birth was celebrated by schoolmasters, not only in

importance of positive religious truth in the education of children, and to maintain that the mere habit of faith and love, if cultivated towards earthly friends and benefactors, would be transferred to our Heavenly Father, whenever His character should be exhibited to the mind of the child. But good cannot come from ignoring the corruption of human nature, nor regeneration take place without being born of the Spirit. There is in human nature not merely blindness of the understanding, but perversity of the will, corruption of the heart, and alienation of the affections, which must be overcome, purified, and restored. This can only be effected by the quickening power of the Gospel, presented, illustrated, applied in the teaching and training of the child, and blessed by the Holy Spirit. It is thus that the Institutions named have taken the educational principles of the Swiss philanthropist, and applied them to a true evangelical training.

his native country, but throughout Germany, it was found that Pestalozzian ideas had been sown, and were bearing fruit over the greater part of Central Europe."—*Quick.*

England has of late also been a seed-plot, and greatly benefited by it.

QUESTIONS ON DR. MAYO'S "LECTURE ON THE LIFE OF PESTALOZZI."

1. What features of character are brought out in Dr. Mayo's portrait of Pestalozzi?

2. What disadvantages did Pestalozzi suffer in early life?

3. How did Pestalozzi propose to benefit the poor?

4. What was the character of Madame Pestalozzi, and what the tokens of affection she received after her death?

5. Infer the character of Lavater from the incidents mentioned respecting him.

6. What was the design of the establishment at Neuhof?

7. What were the causes of Pestalozzi's difficulties at Neuhof, and how did he act amidst them?

8. What effect had the trials and failures of Pestalozzi at Neuhof on his mind and character?

9. What was Pestalozzi's first task on opening his school at Stanz, and how did he accomplish it?

10. How would you characterize Pestalozzi's method of teaching?

11. Under what difficulties did Pestalozzi labour, and how did he meet them?

12. How would you describe the first and second steps of education as given by Pestalozzi?

13. What was the difference between his monitors and those of Bell and Lancaster?

14. What are the first two things to be done in education, and what the advantages of the second of these?

15. What influence had Pestalozzi on his pupils and those around him?

16. How do you account for Pestalozzi's failures, and how do you view his religious opinions?

PART II.

—•—

PESTALOZZI AND HIS PRINCIPLES.

BY

ELIZABETH MAYO.

WITH NOTES, ORIGINAL AND SELECTED,

By ROBERT DUNNING,

FORMERLY LECTURER ON SCHOOL MANAGEMENT, HOME AND COLONIAL TRAINING COLLEGE.

PART II.

PESTALOZZI & HIS PRINCIPLES.

INTRODUCTION.

STRANGE as it may seem, What is Pestalozzianism?
is a question yet to be answered. There are many
who ask, but few can reply to it. The truth is,
that though the history of Pestalozzianism is well
known within a limited circle, and its principles
are becoming appreciated, it has fared with its
author as with many other benefactors of their
species—he has not taken the place which belongs to him in the records of fame; and there
are few men generous enough to anticipate the ver-
dict of posterity, by publishing their secret convictions, at the cost, perhaps, of some immediate
discredit to themselves or their country. Whatever
may be the cause, certain it is that justice has never
yet been done to the individual whose name is
indentified with a new system of teaching. So little
indeed is it known to whom we owe some of the
best parts of our own improvements in education,

much less what Pestalozzianism essentially is, that we believe it would bé quite necessary to begin *ab ovo* with a large class of readers, and retrace the matter historically, in order to acquaint them with its merits. We propose to give a brief answér to the question with which we commenced, by some quotations from approved sources. Our object is to furnish the general features of the system, and enable our readers to recognize it as now, to some extent, adopted, though not indentified with the name of Pestalozzi.

We reply, then, to the inquiry first, that Pestalozzianism is the system of education originating with Pestalozzi, a Swiss philanthropist, who devoted himself with uncommon ardour and self-sacrifice to ameliorate the condition of his poorer countrymen, and that in a moral and intellectual as well as in a physical point of view. In the prosecution of his benevolent object, he became a practical educator, a working schoolmaster ; and hence, perhaps, the ultimate success of his principles.* Though a man

---

* " I will be a schoolmaster ! " he cried ; and a schoolmaster he became. He descended from the Bar, for which he was destined, to the schoolroom. He was an enthusiast, who offered himself on the shrine of teaching, a sacrifice to his country ; not an experimenting amateur, but *con amore*, a professional educator. He practised under circumstances in which not only was speculation put to the test, but necessity became the mother of invention. Many of the

of philosophical mind, he was not a mere theorist or speculator, but one who brought his views to the test of experiment, and, to a great extent, realized them himself by experience, so that the best history of his system would, in fact, be—a history of his personal labours and gradual progress in the practical art of teaching.* The principles of the system

principles he afterwards propounded were arrived at in connection with his practice. Instead of trusting to accident, he threw himself on the broad principles of human nature ; he never mistook machinery for the work to be done—matter for mind, or tools for hands. He was a thoughtful worker, who saw in every act the operation of some principle, and set himself to find it out.

* Miss Mayo, who wrote this little work, being herself intensely practical, hardly gave sufficient prominence to the mental character of Pestalozzi, and, by so largely guarding her hero against theory, seems to forget that but for his philosophical cast of mind we never should have had those great principles of education which are alike our advantage and the characteristic of his system. To whom else, from the days of practical Roger Ascham, through Bell and Lancaster to the equally practical David Stow, can we look for a set of comprehensive principles of education based on the nature, wants, and destiny of man ? The happy hits of blind invention, accidental suggestion, or unregulated ingenuity were in his case matters of elaborated thought, logical deduction, and philosophic generalization ; and a single discovery was with Pestalozzi a matter of order and system. The discoveries of others were the achievements of free lances, his the conquests of a trained and accomplished warrior. He was endowed with keen penetration, the power of analysis, and that of tracing the relations of cause and effect. This he exhibited, both in his analysis of the mental faculties and the subjects of instruction,

F

were, indeed, known and acted upon in times long anterior to his. As one of Her Majesty's Inspectors, Mr. Tremenheere, has well observed, Pestalozzi, in one respect, did but give " a more extensive application to what had been the enlightened practice of former times, and the principles of all the most philosophical writers on the subject of education

He was not a mere observer of mental phenomena, but traced outward manifestations in looks, words, and actions to the sources whence they originated. He considered the mind as a beautiful, intelligent, self-acting machine which throws off all the looks, words, actions that constitute the conduct of man. He felt, also, that to effect any change in the circumstances of man, a change must be produced in the mind or views. It was in connection with such speculations that he took correct views of the source of the *evils* which affected his countrymen, and also of the only *remedy* which would effectually meet the wants of those whom he would serve. Hence his estimate of education as a means of carrying out his aims of creating independence, happiness, and usefulness, and consequently personal and social elevation. Pestalozzi viewed human nature in all its elements, conditions, and wants, and was therefore prepared not to deal with class or temporary emergencies—not for peculiar cases, but for man in all his usual wants and circumstances. In this wide generalization he gave their proper value to the artificial distinctions of society. He saw in them a sufficient number of points of resemblance to constitute them one family, to be subjected to one general regimen, requiring individual and class treatment. He looked at all human beings as possessed of mind, the gift of God, the mainspring of all human activity, destined to live for ever. Thus he descended into the region of thought until he had discovered principles of education which were of universal application.

down to his own day." But this was a high merit; and, let us add, Pestalozzi was no plagiarist. We hardly know whether it is fair to speak of him as having "*received*" these principles. At all events, he was the first to establish and develop them as principles of popular education ; * and he has, we

In submitting his speculations to the test of experiment, there was a rare exhibition of practical good sense. His experiments were not only extensively carried on by himself, but carefully detailed in all their workings by others, upon whose testimony and judgment he could rely. Pestalozzi was as fond of experiment as others are of forming theories or of dogmatizing on mere practice. He was also candid in rejecting all that stood not the fiery ordeal, and possessed only the semblance of truth. When he failed in any of his experiments, he consoled himself with the experience he had gained, and with this fresh light renewed his trials. When he succeeded in any plan, he knew it must be founded on *some principle* of human nature. If the principle was not known to him, he set about finding it out ; if known, he traced the result to the source, which he further established by facts. It appeared ever to be a principle of action with Pestalozzi to conduct his operations in the spirit of science when he could do so, by the light of experience without scientific insight where he could not ; but with a uniform contempt for quackery in all cases. From all this we need not wonder that practical measures have been founded on his principles, and that an Institution, raised up to propagate Pestalozzianism, in its application both to elementary and normal schools, should occupy a high place among the educational establishments of the country.

* Miss Mayo might have added, the first to popularize and apply the abstractions of metaphysics ; the first to take the philosophy of

think, in this respect, a just claim to be regarded as the originator of a system—a system the fruits of which, however co-extensive with the educa- tional movement of the day, appear to us to be far less commonly associated with the name Pestalozzi, at least in this country, than Mr. Tremenheere seems to suppose. The fact is, Pestalozzi's system,

the human mind, and apply it systematically to the education of large numbers—basing the practice of the latter on the principles of the former. Others may have propounded the same principles. Indeed, to our own Locke the Germans are much indebted for their knowledge of mental science; and there is scarcely an educational principle now recognized but might be pointed out in the pages of Locke, Brown, Reid, Hartley, Mill, and others; but none of these writers went beyond theory; if they made any application, as was the case with Hannah More, Elizabeth Hamilton, and Maria Edge- worth, and in the tractates of Milton, they applied it only to home- education and the teaching of a single pupil. The methods of teaching which they adopted, if based on principles, belonged rather to incidental than systematic instruction. It could be easily shown, with respect to this country, that Pestalozzi was the first to define clearly the work of the schoolmaster, to give him the highest aim, and bid him measure his modes of education by it, to inspire him with the right spirit, and enable him to proceed in his work with all the certainty of the light of science. What was given as mere philosophy by some, and partially applied by others, was clearly and fully brought out in the schoolroom of national educa- tion by the Swiss philanthropist. Miss Mayo might also have said that it was the fire of his soul which stirred a flame in Germany and Switzerland whose light has reached our own country, and is con- suming the framework of our old mechanical systems of instruction.

more or less modified, prevails extensively, the principles of it are generally admitted, and their effect felt — Pestalozzi himself is little known, and his labours seldom acknowledged.*

The education of the poorer classes, when Pesta‚ lozzi first propounded his principles, was essentially

As Raumer informs us, " Pestalozzi compelled the scholastic world to revise the whole of their task, to reflect on the nature and destiny of man, and on the proper way of leading him from his youth to that destiny." Quick, borrowing from German sources, declares that, "With the zeal of a Luther he denounced the teaching of his day. 'The present race of schoolmasters,' he writes, 'sacrifice the essence of true teaching to disconnected teaching in a complete jumble of subjects.'"

* Woodbridge, in his "Annals of Education," bears no unfaltering testimony to what Pestalozzi did for the cause. He says :—"He combated with unshrinking boldness and untiring perseverance, through a long life, the prejudices and abuses of the age in reference to education, both by his example and by his numerous publications. He attacked with vigour and success that favourite maxim of bigotry and tyranny, that obedience and devotion are the legitimate offspring of ignorance. He denounced that degrading system which considers it enough to enable man to procure a subsistence for himself and his offspring ; and in this merely to place him on a level with the beast of the forest, deeming everything lost the value of which cannot be estimated in money. He urged upon the consciences of parents the solemn duties which Divine Providence had imposed upon them in committing to their charge the present and future destinies of their fellow-beings. In this way he produced an impulse which pervaded the continent of Europe, and which, by means of his popular and theoretical

defective. In *substance* it consisted in little more
than reading, writing, and the rudiments of arithmetic; while in point of *method* it was almost
purely mechanical, and in *principles* without any
basis of sound science. Hence the head was but
little improved, whilst the heart too often remained
wholly untouched. Education in regard to the

works, reached the cottages of the poor and the palaces of the great.
His Institution at Yverdon was crowded with men of every nation;
not merely those who were led by the same impulse which inspired
him, but by the agents of kings and noblemen and public institutions, who came to make themselves acquainted with his principles
in order to become his fellow-labourers in other countries.

" If we seek for the root of Pestalozzi's system, we shall find it, I
think, in that which was the motive power of Pestalozzi's career,
' the enthusiasm of humanity.' Consumed with grief for the degradation of the Swiss peasantry, he never lost faith in their true
dignity as men, and in the possibility of raising them to a condition
worthy of it. He cast about for the best means of thus raising
them, and decided that it could be effected, not by any improvement in their outward circumstances, but by an education which
should make them what their Creator intended them to be, and
should give them the use and the consciousness of all their inborn
faculties. ' From my youth up,' he says, ' I felt what a high and
indispensable duty it is to labour for the poor and miserable; . . . .
that he may attain to a consciousness of his own dignity through
his feeling of the powers and endowments which he possesses; that
he may not only learn to gabble over by rote the religious maxim,
that " man is created in the image of God, and is bound to live and
die as a child of God," but may himself experience its truth by
virtue of the Divine power within him.' "

masses was indeed an acknowledged failure; nor was it successful in the middle and higher walks of the community. Even here *knowledge* was a great desideratum; and yet often the amount communicated was slight and superficial. Nor were the *methods*, any more than the aim of education, based on any intelligible or consistent principles; such, indeed, were little or not at all recognized; and hence the failure in point of positive results. A system so defective, if system it can be called, must in the nature of things be all but fruitless; and so it proved. Pestalozzi saw and lamented the prevailing errors in education. We believe, too, that he was the first to suggest an adequate remedy; and more than this, he devoted his long life to its illustration and practical application.

THE HISTORY OF PESTALOZZI.

It has been already stated that the best history of Pestalozzi's system would in fact be a history of his personal labours and gradual progress as a practical educator. His principles were so completely worked out by the circumstances in which he was placed, and were so fully the result of successive experiments, that a brief sketch of his life seems quite necessary as a clue to his system. It is proposed, therefore, at the risk of repetition, to notice a few particulars in the history of this remarkable man, and to indicate the more important principles which originated his successful experiments. They are evidently the suggestions of an original mind, and, when viewed in all their detail, exhibit his character in a light peculiarly instructive. He was a man cast in no common mould : drawing as he did from his own resources, possessing a sanguine temperament and a benevolent disposition, he rose superior to disappointments and trials which would have driven ordinary minds to despair. Ridicule, contempt, and, what perhaps is still harder to bear, the basest ingratitude, served only to nerve him for his work, although they detained him longer in the development of his principles, which he had issued in the fullest conviction of their truth, and a firm persuasion that his system, thus tried and proved, must eventually triumph over all impediments.

The birth, parentage, and education of Pestalozzi, as well as his early life and marriage, are adverted to at some length in Dr. Mayo's Memoir, and need not, therefore, be repeated here.

At length Pestalozzi found himself in a condition to carry out, in some measure, the benevolent wishes which he had conceived for the elevation of his

poorer countrymen ; their degraded state touched
his heart, and he longed to raise them in the scale
of humanity.* This led to his first attempts at
Neuhof (so he called his farm), where he endeavoured to work out his ideas as to what National
Education should be. A number of children whom
he had rescued from the most abject poverty were
there formed into a regular establishment, and
initiated in the various branches of rural and domestic economy. A cotton manufactory, also, in which
he was a partner, served to furnish them with additional employment, and enabled him to keep up
industrious habits during the suspension of agricultural labour. All this, however, he considered but
subsidiary; success, he rightly thought, must depend upon the simultaneous use of means of a
higher order ; nor was he unprepared for the more
essential features of his undertaking. Pestalozzi
had acquired a deep insight into the workings of
his own mind, and had, moreover, enjoyed ample
means of watching the mental and moral processes
which so commonly betray the uneducated classes

* The intensity of his benevolence is shown in the following
extract from the Preface to a late edition of " Leonard and Gertrude." He says :—" I desired nothing then, and desire nothing
now, but the welfare of the people, whom I love, and whom I feel
to be miserable, because I have with them borne their sufferings as
few have borne them."

into sin, and render them the dupes of ignorance, prejudice, and vice. Yet he was but a novice in the treatment of those mental diseases which he desired to cure. He had the will, but lacked the experience which the case required. Mere negative wisdom would not suffice for so bold an enterprise. His establishment required to be organized on positive principles, and the principles of Pestalozzi were as yet only faintly defined. But though he did not realize his hopes, his attempt must not be considered a fruitless one. The very failures of Pestalozzi, observes one of his biographers, have proved a **greater** benefit to mankind than the successes of others, and even in this, the first stage of his progress, he established an unquestionable claim to our respect. . .

In his own account of the matter, he says :—

"I had passed some years amongst a circle of more than fifty children, whose parents were in the most abject misery. Poor as I then was, I divided my bread with them ; I lived myself a mendicant, in order to teach mendicants to live like men. The idea which I had formed of the instruction I ought to give them included a knowledge of agriculture, of trades, and of commerce. I had a perfect conviction of the solidity of my plan, and am still of opinion that I am not deceived ; but the truth was,

I wanted a sufficient knowledge of the details necessary in all these three, and I likewise wanted the
talent of devoting myself to those minutiæ which
are necessary to their success ; nor was I sufficiently
rich, and soon found myself too much distressed to
procure what was absolutely requisite to the accomplishment of my enterprise. My plan failed, but
in the midst of the laborious efforts I had made I
learnt innumerable truths ; and I was never more
strongly convinced of the goodness of my project
than at the moment when I found myself obliged
to renounce it."

The consciousness of having saved such a number
of human beings from almost certain destruction,
and of having cherished in their hearts the seeds of
virtue and religion, was no small reward, and yet it
was perhaps the least that Pestalozzi reaped from
his first experiment at Neuhof. He had gained
what was of infinitely greater value to him—a rich
store of experience, and a deeper insight than he
had before possessed into the nature of his task,
and the means by which it was to be accomplished.
He drew out the results of this experience in his
popular tale of " Leonard and Gertrude," a tale
which soon became the delight of his countrymen.
They read it for amusement, they consulted it for
their instruction, and esteemed it, in fact, next to

their Bible. No foreigner can enter fully into its merits, nor will it be enjoyed by any one who looks for a story with a well-arranged plot. A great admirer, however, of Pestalozzi, speaking of it, says:— "There is a truth in the sketching and the colouring of the scenes which more than makes up for the looseness of the thread by which they are strung together; it rivals the faithfulness of the Dutch school of painting, without imitating its laborious accuracy, which mistakes minuteness for variety, and quaintness for originality."

The great principle which Pestalozzi desired to exhibit was, that the amelioration of mankind must commence in the domestic circle. He looked for a power to bring about the bright visions that floated before him, and could think of none commensurate to the work but maternal love—the most powerful of all affections, and the most free from base alloy. Pestalozzi was right: God has committed the child to an influence all-powerful, and great are the mother's responsibilities; but her strength is in Him who has more than a mother's tenderness (Isa. xix. 15); her support is in that Divine assurance which cannot fail (Prov. xxii. 6). A mother is all in all to her dependent child. God has given her the power to administer to its infant wants, and thus she gains the first hold on its affections, and has the opportunity of creating the earliest impressions, always the most indelible. She thus occupies, so to speak, untilled ground, and may sow seed, which, though for a while choked with many weeds, will eventually be sure to germinate and yield fruit. The mother has the opportunity of forming the habits, of bending the supple twig, and she may confidently look to that blessing which will give success to her feeble efforts. We have not the slightest doubt that, were mothers to read and think, so as to acquire the power of doing their duty by their offspring, in humble dependence on God's help, a far greater renovation would be effected than by any other means with which God has been pleased to entrust us.*

To return, however, to Pestalozzi himself (though in truth we have hitherto only spoken his sentiments), he had, it seems, with many other philanthropists, fondly hoped that the French Revolution, by breaking the fetters of oppression and removing trammels which had weighed down the lower orders, would produce a corresponding revolution in their moral and mental condition ; but he soon learnt to recognize as a grand axiom, that " the amelioration of outward circumstances will be the effect, but

---

* See "'The Family Character of the School " in the " Principles of Pestalozzi."

can never be the means, of mental and moral improvement."

Whilst exposed to bitter poverty, and treated as a wild enthusiast, he still carried on the all-absorbing design of his life, and endeavoured, by means of his pen, to disseminate his principles. The circumstances which brought him to Stanz, together with his first experiments there, have been given in the Memoir.

" The first benefit which Pestalozzi derived from the hard necessity of his position at Stanz, was that he saw himself stripped of all the ordinary props of authority, and in a manner compelled to rely upon the power of love in the child's heart as the only source of obedience : an all-forbearing kindness was the magic he used to gain ascendancy over his pupils." He was thus, in matters of discipline, reduced to the primary motive (Rom. xiii. 10) of all virtue. Pestalozzi also learned, in the attempt to educate under such peculiar circumstances, the art of simplification in matters of instruction. " He was entirely unprovided with books, or any means of instruction ; and in the absence of both material and machinery, he could not have recourse even to the pursuits of industry for filling up part of the time. The whole of his school apparatus consisted of himself and his pupils ; and he was, there-

fore, compelled to investigate what means these would
afford him for the accomplishment of his end. The
result was that he learnt the art of returning to the
simplest elements, he abstracted himself from all those
artificial elements of instruction contained in books,
and directed his whole attention to the materials in
the child's mind. He taught numbers instead of
cyphers, living sounds instead of dead characters,
deeds of faith and love instead of abstruse creeds,
substances instead of shadows, realities instead of
signs. He led the intellect of the children to the
discovery of truths which, in the nature of things, they
could never forget, instead of burdening their memory
with the recollection of words, which, in the nature of
things, they could not understand. Instead of building up a dead mind and a dead heart, on the ground
of the dead letter, he drew forth life to the mind and
life to the heart by working from within."

Absorbed in supplying the necessities of the
moment, and " standing in the midst of his children, he forgot that there was any world besides
his asylum. And as their circle was a universe
to him, so was he to them all in all. From morning to night he was the centre of their existence.
To him they owed every comfort and every enjoyment; and whatever hardships they had to endure,
he was their fellow-sufferer. He partook of their

meals, and slept amongst them. In the evening he prayed with them before they went to bed, and from his conversation they dropped into the arms of slumber. At the first dawn of light it was his voice that called them to the light of the rising sun and to the praise of their heavenly Father. All day he stood amongst them, teaching the ignorant, assisting the helpless, encouraging the weak, and admonishing the transgressor. His hand was daily with them, joined in theirs ; his eye, beaming with benevolence, beamed on theirs. He wept when they wept, and rejoiced when they rejoiced. He was to them a father, and they were to him as children. Such love could not fail to win their hearts ; the most savage and the most obstinate could not resist the soothing influence. Discontent and peevishness ceased, and a number of between seventy and eighty children, whose dispositions had been far from kind, and their habits anything but domestic, were thus converted in a short time into a peaceable domestic circle, in which it was a delight to dwell." *

The picture of a schoolmaster, in his " Leonard and Gertrude," is quite in harmony with his own conduct. . . . " Gluelphi knew that confidence and affection for human benefactors are the stepping-

* See the "Life of Pestalozzi," by the Rev. Dr. Biber.

stones for the child to those more elevated feelings of faith and love with which he ought to embrace the Supreme Being, and he made it a leading object of his solicitude to guide the children's minds to perceive the manifold evidences of goodness and mercy towards them manifested in the occurrences of daily life and the experiences of their own hearts.

" He was deeply impressed with the truth, that moral education is not so much impressed by words as facts.

" For kindling in their souls the flame of love and devotion, he trusted not to the hearing and learning of passages setting forth the beauties of love and its blessings, but he endeavoured to mani-fest to them a spirit of genuine piety, and to en-courage them to the practice of it, both by precept and example. . . . He led them to live in love ; he presented to their minds the distresses of others —not of men who had lived thousands of years before them, but of those who were near them, whose tears they saw flowing, in whose emaciated countenances they could themselves read the in-scription of hunger, whose nakedness and helpless-ness made an immediate appeal to their senses. . . . By the sight of misery, he endeavoured to excite commiseration in the hearts of the children, and to lead them to reflect on the causes of distress and

G

suffering, and on the means of alleviating them. He rendered them attentive to the afflictions of their fellow-creatures, and especially of those who were connected with them by any nearer ties, for he knew that the sympathies of life are most acutely felt in the circle of the family.

" If there were some one ill in the houses of any of the children, were it a father or mother, a brother or sister, or even the meanest servant, he never failed to ask the child the moment he entered the schoolroom how the invalid was, and the child had to give a detailed and accurate account. Gluelphi did not take half answers on such occasions, but was so particular in his inquiries, that if the child had not asked the sick person, he would at once betray his inattention, and be overwhelmed with such confusion, that he would certainly never so offend again. The children were also asked if they had themselves spoken to the invalid, and whether they had contributed to alleviate his sufferings, if it were only by avoiding all noise and bustle in the house.* Of the dear children Gluelphi inquired

---

* An excellent hint for the moral discipline of our infant schools. A similar spirit we recollect to have seen manifested by a mistress who had been trained at the Home and Colonial Training Schools in Gray's Inn Road. One of the children of her school had met with an accident, and was sent to a hospital. When dismissed, she was recommended to live upon

whether they sat up with the sick, and how long they could bear it, and he testified his approbation when they did it willingly. Nor did he ever omit the question, 'Do you pray every morning and evening for your invalid, that God may restore him to health?'"

Conscious of the benefits he had himself derived from his domestic education, Pestalozzi was anxious to give to his Asylum the character of a family rather than of a public school. He frequently entertained his children with descriptions of a happy and well-regulated household, and endeavoured to bring them to a lively sense of the blessings which man may bestow upon man by the exercise of mutual Christian love. But on this, as on all other subjects, he taught as much or more by his life and practice than by his words.

When the neighbouring village of Altorf was destroyed by fire, Pestalozzi assembled his flock around him, and addressed them, "Children, Altorf lies in ashes. Do you recollect the day when you first came here, in want of everything, some of you shivering with cold, others suffering from disease,

milk, but the parents were too poor to afford all she required. The teacher told the case to her school-fellows, and it was pleasing to see how much she collected every week in pence and farthings to help the poor sufferer.

others subject to ill-treatment, but all without a feeling of affection for others, or of happiness within yourselves? Such are the children of the Altorfers this day. You feel happy; you have the benefit of useful instruction; you take pleasure in what is good."

In the conversations of Pestalozzi with his children, and the appeal which he made to them on the destruction of the town of Altorf, already described in the Memoir, we have set forth Pestalozzi's views of moral education. " His principle was to awaken the feeling, then to give it a name, and when it was alive, to substantiate it as a rule of action."

The account he gives his friend Gessner of his first efforts to reduce his wild undisciplined children to something like order, and to bring their powers into activity, and awaken their sympathies, is so interesting that we quote his own words :—
" Through Legrand, I made some interest with the first Directoire for the subject of popular education, and I was preparing to open an extensive establishment for that purpose in Argau, when Stanz was burnt down, and Legrand requested me to make the scene of misery the first scene of my operations. I went—I would have gone into the remotest clefts of the mountains to come nearer to my aim—and now I *did* come nearer. But imagine

my position : alone, destitute of all means of instruction, and of all other assistance, I united in my person the offices of superintendent, paymaster, steward, and sometimes chambermaid, in a half-ruined house. I was surrounded with ignorance, disease, and every kind of novelty. The number of children rose by degrees to eighty, all of different ages ; some full of pretensions, others inured to open beggary; and all, with a few solitary exceptions, entirely ignorant. What a task, to educate, to develop these children !—what a task !

" I ventured upon it. I stood in the midst of these children pronouncing various sounds, and asking them to imitate them. Whoever saw it was struck with the effect. It is true it was a meteor which vanishes in the air as soon as it appears. No one understood its nature. I did not understand it myself. It was the result of a simple idea, or rather a fact, of human nature, which was revealed to my feelings, but of which I was far from having a clear consciousness."

Dr. Biber makes the following useful remarks on the plan adopted by Pestalozzi :—

'The simultaneous production of sounds which was Pestalozzi's first, and no doubt a most judicious, means for assimilating a mass of heterogeneous elements, has been adopted with similar success in the first establishment of infant schools, and has since acquired a sort of popularity, which has greatly accelerated the evil, almost inevitable, of its being turned into an abuse. It seems, therefore, well to examine its nature, in order to ascertain what connection it has with the Pestalozzian plan of education, of which it has been made by some the main prop. The first and most obvious feeling aroused by a simultaneous act of any sort, is that of unity. Thence the pleasing effect which the simultaneous movement of a regiment of soldiers produces. Also the impressive effect of the responses, when followed up by the whole congregation, is, in a great measure, to be referred to this feeling of delight in unison of any kind. A taste for unison not only becomes more intense in proportion to the number of individuals united, but it also gains in depth and refinement when the higher and nobler faculties of our being are called into simultaneous action. A general clapping of hands is one of the favourite exercises of an infant school, and the sound of a thousand feet stamping the ground at one instant enchants the ears of an uncultivated youth, and prompts him to join his supernumerary limbs with those of the marching regiment.

" But the sound of our voices is a far more powerful means of expressing our feelings than the motion of our limbs; and accordingly, the simple, uniform repetition of any, even the most monotonous and unmeaning sounds, is music to the ears of children and savages, while the hauling of an anchor is materially facilitated by the sailors' call. The measuring of time and its uniform division, is an indispensable condition of every simultaneous movement; and as an intellectual operation, though of the very lowest kind, it forms an essential ingredient of the internal delight which the movement produces. This intense delight is increased, if to the harmony of time that of tone be added; and in their joint effect consists the deep charm of music. The value of music, again, is raised, if, with its sounds, the feelings of kindred affections, or the higher ones of adoration, be associated in simultaneous expression; and abstracting itself from all that is external, or addressing itself to the senses, nothing can be more ravishing than the idea of myriads of spirits, whose deepest and unuttered thoughts are united in an everlasting harmony of love and praise to the Father of spirits.

" Such is the effect of one and the same feeling at different stages of human development. Its powerful influence is manifest; its tendency cannot be condemned, because it is met with wherever man is progressing towards good; and we find him shrinking from it into selfish shyness whenever he is conscious of evil. The question, then, is for us, What use is to be made of it in education? This depends entirely upon the stage of develop- ment which the children have attained. With such as have grown up in a condition almost savage, and who are, for the first time, brought together under an influence intended for their improvement, the lowest degree of simultaneous action is. calculated to arouse the soul from the selfish indolence in which it loves nothing and observes nothing but self. For this purpose Pestalozzi made his chil- dren pronounce sounds together, and his ' meteoriç ' success was the natural effect of the lever which he brought into action. But had he stopped there, as many of his pretended disciples have done—had he continued to pronounce sounds and elicit their simultaneous imitation, his experiment would have terminated as the sound vanished amongst his mountains. But Pestalozzi was too wise to commit such a mistake ; his narrative shows how he availed himself of the success of this first experiment for the attainment of more important objects.

"It ought to be a rule with a teacher never to employ this means for bringing a new subject before his pupils, or inculcating anything which they did not previously know, but to confine its use exclusively to repetition. Thus, supposing the lesson to be the analysis of the first numbers, the teacher, having led the children by making strokes on the slates to see that two is one and one—three, two and one, or one and two, will then call upon them simultaneously to repeat what they had observed. Whoever will take the trouble to reflect on the effect which this mode of proceeding must produce upon children's minds will easily discover the difference between the simultaneous repetition of a lesson produced by the children themselves, and the mere inculcation, through the ear, of a lesson with which their own minds have never grappled. To such it will be apparent that the simultaneous repetition, whether in a musical form or not, of addition, multiplication, pence, weight, and other tables, now so common in public schools, so far from forming a part of Pestalozzi's plan, is, on the contrary, a mere caricature of it."

From these quotations we may learn what were some of the first principles struck out by Pestalozzi as a practical educator. Let us now picture him to our minds surrounded by his family at Stanz, showing how a number of once lawless rebels may be won by love, and reduced by a course of patient and judicious discipline to habits of order and obedience, and we shall be the better able to fully trace the unfolding of his principles, and watch the working out of his system. We have seen how, by the attraction of a self-denying love, and the powerful influence of sympathy, he had brought under subjection the lawless little band that composed his school, and under the bright beams of his own benevolence had cherished feelings and sentiments that elevated their characters.

His next problem was, how to educate their minds. It was, perhaps, favourable to his after success that he was, as before observed, deprived of the usual machinery of the schoolmaster, and thereby thrown on the resources of his own great mind. Thus circumstanced, he was led to consider essential principles, to study the child himself, his wants, his capabilities, his tendencies, and his habits. The first step in his theory was to view education as an organic development—the unfolding of germs within the child, not the deposition of something from without. He also saw the analogy between our physical and mental constitution, and that the food presented to either, in order to convey due nourishment, must be suited to its powers, that the work of digestion and assimilation may be carried on.*

Wherever Pestalozzi saw a land-mark, thither he

* The "organic character" of education based on this principle will be found further on in this volume.

steered his course ; thus he soon perceived the ever-busy working of the senses in early childhood, and the vivid conceptions of truth that resulted from an intimate acquaintance with things themselves. Here, then, was his first guide—he broke through the exclusive dominion of words in education, and required a knowledge of the thing signified, before he gave its sign or name. He also cultivated the moral perceptions of his scholars by means of actions and events that passed under their own observation, whilst the material world around them formed the ground-work of their intellectual development. The account of the first introduction of lessons on objects is thus given by one whom Pestalozzi delighted to honour as his friend, and to whom he communicated the details of his various experiments. The Rev. Dr. Mayo writes in his Preface to " Lessons on Objects ":—

" This mode of instruction was suggested to the mind of Pestalozzi by the peculiar circumstances in which he was placed at Stanz. The brutalized state into which the children confided to his care had fallen rendered it absolutely necessary to find some new mode of interesting their minds and calling out their dormant faculties.

" Nature was the only book with which they were conversant, and their first lessons were consequently drawn from its pages. Experience and judgment retained what necessity first imposed. The subjects ordinarily presented to the youthful mind appeared too remote from that knowledge which the child acquires without regular instruction, and were generally taught in too abstract a manner. It was proposed to bring education more into contact with the child's own experience and observation, and to find in *him* the first link in the chain of his instruction. In the execution of this plan a series of engravings was provided, representing those objects which are familiar to children, and the lessons consisted in naming their parts, describing their structure and use. One day, however, the master having presented to his class the engraving of a ladder, a lively little boy exclaimed, ' But there is a real ladder in the court-yard; why not talk about it, rather than the picture!' 'The engraving is here,' said the master, 'and it is more convenient to talk about what is before your eyes than to go into the court-yard to talk about the other.' The boy's observation thus eluded was for that time disregarded. Soon after, the engraving of a window formed the object of examination: 'But why,' exclaimed the same little objector, 'why talk of this picture of a window, when there is a real window in the room, and there is no need to go into the court-yard for it?' Again the remark was silenced; but in the evening both circumstances were mentioned to Pestalozzi. 'The boy is right,' said he, 'the reality is better than the counterfeit. Put away the engravings, and let the class be instructed by means of real objects.'" The plan was adopted, and it has produced a great revolution in elementary education—greater, perhaps, than any other change which has been yet adopted.

We are not to suppose that the benefit of this kind of instruction consists in the amount of information that children may acquire, though positive knowledge is not to be despised; but it is the development of an innate power, the formation of an abiding habit, that constitutes its true value. It is difficult to calculate the advantage accruing to the poorer classes, to the mechanic and labourer of all descriptions, by training them to pass through life with eyes to see and ears to hear, to be content with nothing less than precision and accuracy in their mental processes, and by furnishing them also with an extension of their vocabulary, as the range of their ideas enlarges. Object teaching is also beneficial, inasmuch as the impressions made are so distinct and vivid that, through the aid of the imagination and memory, the child enjoys the picture of the object transmitted by the eye to the

mind, when it no longer strikes upon that organ :
and *that*, even with the same vividness as when it
was present. Pestalozzi, in consequence, sought to
lay a foundation for clearness of conception and to
form the judgment of the child by speaking to its
eyes. It also formed the first step of a progressive
course of instruction. It was a fundamental principle with Pestalozzi to commence with what is
most easy, and, before proceeding onward, to be
sure that the child was master of the preceding
steps. Thus he advanced without leaps and without
gaps. The new idea flowed necessarily from the one
just acquired ; and what was the foundation of
instruction (the knowledge of the thing itself)
was immediately and closely connected with the
knowledge of the word by which it was expressed.
No one will deny but that this is truly philosophical, for it is based on the recognized phenomena
of the human mind. It is an acknowledged fact,
that the mind is furnished originally through the
operation of the senses ; and we find that upon the
force and power with which first ideas and impressions are seized will depend almost invariably
the future success of instruction. If the materials
with which we work are imperfect, how can the
result prove satisfactory ? If the objects of perception have either not been noticed, or noticed

imperfectly, by the child, those of conception and judgment must ever be obscure and unsatisfactory. There is, however, one point on which the followers of Pestalozzi need to be cautioned—that is, not to detain the child too long in leading-strings, and to take care that, whilst the steps of instruction are carefully graduated, that are, at the same time, sufficiently distant from each other to require a vigorous effort to pass from one to another. If all be made too easy, too accessible, if the fresh knowledge to be acquired lies quite on the surface, power and vigour will not be exercised. What is obtained with small effort and labour neither strengthens the mind in its acquisition nor retains its hold on the memory.*

---

* This mode of teaching is that which best secures attention and interest in the infant school, and constitutes nearly the whole of its teaching. It is that which distinguishes the lessons given to the infants from those adopted with the juveniles, whose teaching is principally logical ; and we all know with what difference of result, both as to intelligence and happiness, thanks to the disciples of Pestalozzi who introduced it, and who made thorough and systematic what had been but partial in the hands of Wilderspin and his coadjutors in the early days of infant teaching. The intuitive method of teaching moreover prepares the mind for the profitable study of books. However the practice of some so-called Pestalozzian teachers may appear to contradict it, Pestalozzi was no enemy to books and book-learning. It was to their too early introduction he objected. He knew that when the education of a child commences with books

But we should not be doing justice to this subject if we omitted to point out the *moral* effect that is produced on the character from the certainty and precision of the ideas and knowledge gained by the investigation and observation of the pupils themselves. This did not escape the penetration of that acute observer, Madame de Staël, who thus speaks of the system in her work on Germany :—

" Pestalozzi considers rightly that there is a moral satisfaction in completeness in our studies. Superficial knowledge leads continually to the artful concealment of our ignorance, and candour suffers from all the defects of instruction which

the mind gets loaded with words that convey no definite meaning, or meaning unsuitable to the period of infancy. The consequence is that the powers of the mind are cramped instead of being enlarged. In the prizes first awarded by Lord Ashburton for excellence in the knowledge of "Common Things," and in the able advocacy of the *Times* newspaper of the same subject, we see a due appreciation of one branch of intuitive teaching. And thus, however unconsciously, the English nobleman and the English journalist become the followers of the Swiss schoolmaster and philanthropist. The impetus given some time ago to the subject of object-teaching has lost much of its power. This is accounted for without suspecting the method of dealing with the subject. Teachers neglected the subjects which parents and others most appreciated, the cry of over-educating was got up, and we know with what result. It culminated in the Commissioners of Education recommending that in reading, writing, and arithmetic alone should children be examined. A better state of things now exists.

give rise to the feeling of shame. To know perfectly what is known communicates a repose to the
mind nearly resembling satisfaction of conscience.
The truthfulness and integrity of Pestalozzi, an
integrity carried into the sphere of intelligence,
and which deals with ideas as scrupulously as with
men, is one of the principal merits of his school."
The same idea of the moral influence that results
from the system of intellectual culture pursued by
Pestalozzi is so well set forth by Mr. Kay Shuttleworth and Mr. Tufnell, in the " Minutes of the
Council on Education," that we cannot refrain
from quoting their opinion. " Pestalozzi," it is
observed, "was careful to devise lessons on objects
in which, by actual contact with the senses, the
children were led to discern qualities which they
afterwards described in words. Such lessons have
no meaning to persons who are satisfied with instruction by rote, but we contend that it is important to a right *moral* state of the intelligence that
the child should have a clear perception and
vivid *conviction* of every fact presented to the mind.
We are of opinion, that to extend the province of
faith and implicit, unreasoning obedience to those
subjects which are the proper objects on which the
perceptive faculties ought to be exercised, and on
which the reason should be employed, is to undermine

H

the basis of an unwavering faith in revelation, by provoking the rebellion of the human spirit against authority in matters in which reason is free.

"To the young the truth (bare before the sight, palpable to the touch, embodied in forms which the senses realize) has a charm which no mere words can convey, until they are recognized as the signs of the truth which the mind comprehends. In all that relates to the external phenomena of the world, the best book is Nature, with an intelligent inter-preter. What concerns the social state of man may be best apprehended after lessons in the fields, the ruins, the mansions, and the streets within reach of the school. Lessons on the individual objects prepare the mind for generalization, and for the exercise of faith in its proper province. The elementary schools in which *word*-teaching only exists do not produce earnest and truthful men." *

As the result of some of Pestalozzi's experiments at Stanz, certain fundamental points gradually estab-lished themselves in his mind, and guided him in the

---

* The great difference between Stow's system and that of Pestalozzi is, that the former educates by *words;* language is the means he uses for mental training. Pestalozzi educated by *things* and realities, and cultivated language to give the power of expressing ideas thus gained, and of fixing them in the memory, rendering them available for use.

further pursuit of his object. He became every day more convinced that reasoning with children at an early age does no good whatever, but that the only way to a real development of their mental faculties was—1. To enlarge gradually the sphere of their intuition. 2. To impress the perceptions they gained with certainty, clearness, and precision ; and 3. To teach them to express these accurately.

As these three leading points were fixing themselves on his mind, he also began to understand more clearly the means of accomplishing his task. 1. He found, he tells us, that intuitive books for elementary instruction were indispensable. 2. That the method of elucidation traced out in these books must be distinguished by clearness and precision. 3. That upon the ground of the knowledge of things, gained in the order and manner prescribed by these books, the children must be led to a knowledge of names or words, and exercised in the use of them until they acquired ease and propriety of expression.*

* In these paragraphs we have proofs of the ever-active mind of Pestalozzi and the history of one of the leading principles of his system, "That education should be based on intuition." It is not always easy to understand what Pestalozzi means by intuition, but his leading idea was that the child should be taught as much as possible by his own examination of things, instead of his knowledge being founded

Surely it must be interesting to all who have any concern in the improvement of the rising generation thus to watch the progress of an establishment formed of the most unpromising subjects, and deficient in all the materials usually considered essential to the carrying on of education. Yet under such circumstances it was that Pestalozzi enunciated his great principles, and showed to the

on hearsay evidence. This he called intuitive knowledge; the method by which the teacher led his pupil to acquire this knowledge, the intuitive method ; and the manuals by which the teacher was to be guided in the course of his instruction, intuitive books. This is obvious and is equivalent to object teaching, the teaching of things or realities, as described in the Life of Pestalozzi by Dr. and Miss Mayo. But intuitive teaching must not be considered as confined to mere object teaching. By intuition, Pestalozzi meant clear and immediate perception or contemplation of the subject to be learnt, whether grammar, arithmetic, geography, geometry, or arts and manufactures, as well as the mere common object. Pestalozzi, in the early stages of his instruction, substituted the thing for the idea, objects for descriptions and definitions—numbers exhibited in objects or abstractions for cyphers—language in its living,sounds, and practical application, for grammar in its vagueness—musical sounds for notes and the science of music—topography for geography—the forms of objects for the abstractions of geometry—actions, events, and incidents taking place around the child, for the records of the distant and past. Thus the child did not talk about a subject, but was brought face to face with it. " Pestalozzi led the intellect of the children to the discovery of truth, instead of burdening their memories with the recollection of words. Substances were

world how comprehensive a work true education
is. He had the satisfaction at Stanz to see intellectual and moral development proceeding together
and aiding each other. "The details of life," he
tells us, "furnished the means of moral training."
By them he taught his children the difference between good and evil—between what was just and
what was unjust; and, while directing their judg-

taught instead of shadows, and realities for signs. In instruction of
a moral character Pestalozzi taught from actions and events
regarded in a moral light, instead of delivering abstract definitions
and inculcating general truths."—*Biber*. His motto was, "deeds
or facts, not words," deeds of faith and love, instead of abstruse
creeds. Actions are to moral, what objects are to intellectual
instruction. In the study of objects children acquire clear
ideas of the properties of matter, as of transparency and
brittleness in glass, porosity and absorbency in sponge, so by
the consideration of actions witnessed they may be led to
form correct notions of moral qualities, such as justice, generosity, courage, selfishness, &c. Instruction conducted thus
is intuitive moral instruction. It is thus when the teacher
of botany exhibits a plant, or the drawing of a plant, in
illustration of his lecture, and the professor of chemistry
performs his experiment before his class. What the plant is to
botanical science and the experiment is to chemical science, that
an action is to morals. The Pestalozzian teacher of ethics
introduces actions, that his pupils may observe them, determine
their character, trace the motives and dispositions whence they
originated, and thus prepare them for those Christian principles
which should regulate their conduct. This is moral education
based on intuition. Learning by intuition is no more than

ment, he at the same time allowed them a liberty of action that created in them a mode of thinking, uniting solidity with independence. He gave them instruction in geography and natural history, and he adds, " It was most interesting to see the cor rectness of idea and quickness of apprehension with which they applied the particular facts already formed by their experience to general ideas, and to the technical words which represented those ideas."

" This essay convinced me," he says, "that by the simple process which I pursued, I could complete with them a course which would embrace on one side all that was essential to man in ordinary life, and, on the other, would give a child, gifted by nature with many brilliant talents, a sufficient foundation to pursue it further by himself. This system of instruction had the advantage of leav-

---

learning by *experience.* Yet self-evident as is the fact that children learn better from the experience of things than from words, it remained for the Swiss educator to make this distinction with respect to school learning, and practically to introduce it. Experience is the school of wisdom, says the practical Englishman, applying the saying to men and the world. Experience is the school of wisdom alike for children and men, for school and the world, say the followers of Pestalozzi. Thus Pestalozzianism is, in one of its phases, merely a new application of what is thoroughly English in its character.

ing every one in the proper sphere and condition in which he was born; a circumstance, in
my mind, infinitely advantageous to the individual
and to society at large; and it is at the same
time the most certain mode of discovering and
appreciating talents."

Whilst Pestalozzi was most anxious to preserve
the idea of his system, he was compelled to mould
his plans to the peculiar circumstances in which he
was placed; thus we find that the necessity of his
situation led him to devise the plan of *mutual
instruction*, though in an informal manner. It is,
however, highly interesting to observe how he made
it harmonize with his views, and how different an
instrument it was in his hands from what it often
proves in those of the mere routine teacher, who
goes so far to reduce education to a complete
machine. The account of the introduction of this
practice, of the principle on which it was founded, and
of the spirit in which it was carried out has been
given in the Memoir, and need not be repeated.

We have seen that Pestalozzi's mind teemed with
great ideas, and his heart overflowed with benevolence; also, that success was attending his labours.
But the course of greatness is never a smooth or
an even one. It needs, perhaps, as vegetation does,
the chilling blast to retard as well as the fostering

sun to ripen. Adverse gales soon reached the
rising institution at Stanz, and, at the expiration
of a short year, another political crisis obliged
Pestalozzi to abandon his work, and drove him forth
once more without a home, without pupils, and
almost without hope. Thus was he a second time
obliged to abandon a sphere of usefulness, just as
his plans began to mature, and his first crude and
indistinct theories to assume a definite and practical character. Worn out by the incessant exertions he had made, and depressed in spirit by the
sad blighting of his fondest hopes, he retired for a
season to some baths in the neighbourhood of Berne
to recruit his exhausted powers. But it was not
possible for him long to remain inactive. He possessed, in a remarkable degree, that buoyant elas-
ticity of spirit which rebounds with increased
energy at every fall. Conscious of his power, and
convinced of the goodness of his system, he never
abandoned hope, but was ready to adopt any means
likely to subserve the great purpose to which he had
devoted the energies of his powerful mind. It was
a great object—the amelioration of the state and
condition of the poor by means of an improved
system of education! If the warrior who saves his
country from the degradation of a foreign yoke, if
the statesman who raises her by his wise govern-

ment in the scale of nations, deserves his country's gratitude and praise—surely he who spends his life as Pestalozzi did, in working upon the people themselves—who seeks, not so much to alter their circumstances, as to elevate them as intellectual and moral beings—deserves to have his name enrolled amongst the greatest benefactors of mankind.

The next arena of Pestalozzi's exertions was one of the public schools at Bergdorf. But here he was associated with a colleague most uncongenial to his character—a mere mechanical drudge, who, wedded to the old system, jealous of Pestalozzi, and fearing, not only that his own teaching would fall into disrepute, but that he might be superseded in his office, used his utmost endeavours to alarm the parents by detailing the novelties pursued by Pestalozzi, and in this way he at last succeeded in ejecting him.

We next find Pestalozzi happy to teach even in a dame's infant school. What greater proof can we have of the unselfish philanthropy and the beautiful simplicity of this truly great man ? Some may, indeed, smile at Pestalozzi crowing, as he describes it, the A, B, C, from morning to night, with this infant assembly ; but we recognize in it that fixedness of purpose and that ruling passion which led him to consider nothing a degradation that tended to the one great end which he had in view. Soon after this, the

Swiss Government, which was not altogether insensible to the work he had carried on at Stanz, granted him the Castle of Bergdorf for a teachers' seminary, by means of which it was proposed to put the public instruction of the whole country upon an uniform plan. A brighter hope of success seemed now to smile upon him. He was, however, encompassed with difficulties; though possessed of a *locale*, he had no pecuniary means for carrying on his schools. Still he hoped, by the help of a boarding-school for the middle and higher classes, to meet, in part, the expenses of his poorer establishment: his teachers' seminary, he expected, would be established at the expense of the Helvetic Government, as soon as their finances (exhausted by the calamities of war) should render it possible. Another of his plans was, to communicate to the public the result of his researches and experiments, and to furnish various manuals for the use of teachers and parents.

PESTALOZZI'S COADJUTORS.

Happily he was just now joined in his undertaking by men whose heart swelled with the same noble desire for the improvement of education, and who had the same readiness to sacrifice their own

personal interests for the good of others.* It is
true they brought little of scholastic lore to their
work ; but there was a freshness and freedom that
better fitted them to receive the views of another,
whilst they possessed sufficient natural talents to
render them valuable auxiliaries.† All seemed to

* The following fact among others shows the spirit of self-denial
and the high moral interest with which the first followers of Pesta
lozzi embraced his cause.   In addition to the small annuity which
the Helvetic Government voted to Pestalozzi, they granted a stipend
of £25 each to two of his assistants, Krusi and Buss, who, con-
sidering the pressure of Pestalozzi's position, had generosity enough
to appropriate it to the general funds of the house, from which they
received nothing except board and lodging.   The possibility on
Pestalozzi's part of accepting such sacrifices from those who were,
according to the common notions of the world, his employed servants, reflects more credit on his character than the greatest benefits .
which he could have bestowed upon them.   What must have been
the moral ascendency, the intrinsic humility, of a man whose dignity
did not suffer from being supported by those who had a right to
look to him for a remuneration of their services !   He had a greater
reward to give than the wages of Mammon, and it was for that
reward that his disciples served him.   In this they only followed his
example, who—though his new establishment imposed upon him
care and anxiety ill to be endured by a mind like his—was yet overflowing with gratitude to Providence for the opportunity afforded
him of giving a more extensive trial to his views and developing the
principles which he had discovered.

† Among the numbers of literary men from all countries who
at a subsequent period repaired to Pestalozzi's establishment,
many were too wise in their own conceits to enter into the

smile for a short time, the tide of popularity turned in his favour, and many who could not discover the stamp of genius under the lowly guise that obscured it were now ready enough, when the merit of Pestalozzi was acknowledged, to add their meed of praise to the general stock.

His own hopes, however, were mostly centred in the help he obtained from his coadjutors, and he expected, with their assistance, to work out his

methods and principles of Pestalozzi. They could not descend so low as to look to the elements of knowledge as a source of information for themselves. They merely gave a scrutinizing look at the new manner in which those elements were presented, either because they wished to form an opinion on the subject, or their circumstances compelled them to get their bread by the inculcation of those elements. They took a scrap here and there with them to be "grafted in" upon their own system. But the scraps are nothing, and no scholar ever reached the principles unless he first threw his artifical wisdom overboard. However valuable may have been the services rendered subsequently to the cause of Pestalozzi by a few scholars like Dr. Mayo, who consented to become ignorant that they might be made wise; and however great the advantages which these men themselves derived from knowledge previously acquired, by turning it to account as raw material for the practical purposes of the method, still it must be recognized as a most providential arrangement that Pestalozzi was not at the onset of his experiment embarrassed by the assistance of men who "knew something," but that he was surrounded by those who, conscious of their ignorance, were ready to be taught with him by the "mouth of the babes" whom they had undertaken to teach.

system. We will abridge from his letters the account he gives of these good men, and the impression his method made upon them.

Krusi was the first who joined him. He had, in his boyhood, carried on for his father a pretty traffic with neighbouring villages and towns, and thus acquired a knowledge of men and manners, the fruit of that practical kind of observation which often, in the humbler classes of society, lays the foundation for an extended intellectual culture, and gives to its possessor a general acuteness which fits him for success in any future undertakings.

At the age of eighteen he took charge of a village school in the Canton of Appenzel. He was altogether unprepared for this work, but he loved children ; and, thirsting himself for knowledge, he hoped to learn by teaching others. In a few weeks he found himself at the head of a hundred scholars, and then he realized the difficulties of his position. He knew of no plan but that of setting them tasks to learn by heart ; but whilst he was employed with a few, he found the greater number wasting their time and energies in listlessness or folly. Though he soon satisfied the parents by his efforts in teaching them to read and write, he was conscious that he was not cultivating their minds. With the assistance of the Rector of the parish, he commenced questioning his children upon the passages they read, to see if they understood their meaning. He succeeded by this means in making them familiar with what they read, but it did not exercise their judgment or powers of thought, for he adapted his questions to answers that the children readily found in the words of the book. It was, in fact, a mere analysis of words, relieving the child, as far as words were concerned, from the confusion of an unbroken sentence, the different parts being presented separately. The only merit of such questioning is to prepare the mind for a consideration of the ideas themselves which the words convey. Krusi afterwards endeavoured to combine this exercise with the Socratic method, which takes up the subject in a higher sense. But it was not for uncultivated or superficial minds to dive into those depths from which Socrates derived spirit and truth, and, therefore, it was no more than might have been expected that the young unlearned schoolmaster did not succeed in the new system of questioning. He had no internal basis for his questions, nor had the children any for their answers.

"Krusi had not then a clear insight into the nature of those two methods, which might have enabled him to apprehend their difference. He had not learned that mere catechizing, especially if it runs upon abstract terms, leads to no more than the art of separating sentences into words and handling analytical forms, and is often a parrot repetition of sounds without understanding; nor was he aware that Socratic questions are not to be addressed to such pupils as his, equally destitute of the internal fund,—that is, of real knowledge,—and of the external means,—that is, of language wherein to convey that knowledge. The failure of the attempt rendered him unjust to himself; he thought the fault lay entirely in himself. The more he laboured, the more the mountain which he was attempting to climb appeared to elevate its summit above his reach, and the less adequate did he feel himself to attempt its ascent."

It was, however, just this failure that prepared Krusi to appreciate the work of Pestalozzi. He was at this time greatly struck with a conversation on popular education at which he was present, and in the course of which Pestalozzi was explaining that it was not his intention to bring children to a premature judgment on any subject—but that he rather endeavoured to check their judgment until they had the opportunity of viewing the subject from all sides, and under a variety of circumstances, and were perfectly familiar with the words expressive of its nature. The remarks of Pestalozzi led

Krusi to see where his error lay, and he found that
he himself stood in need of the elementary instruction he designed for his children. Krusi's patron
had endeavoured to initiate him in many branches
of science, that he might be able to teach them;
but Krusi felt every day more forcibly that the
method of teaching by books did not suit him,
because he found himself at every line deficient in
that preliminary knowledge of things and their
names, which, more or less, books presuppose. The
consciousness he thus happily acquired of his own
inefficiency, was confirmed when he witnessed the
effects produced by Pestalozzi on his pupils, by
awakening their observation, leading them back to
the first elements of knowledge, and dwelling on
those elements with unwearied patience. "He
perceived," says Pestalozzi, "that the tendency of
my teaching was to develop the internal power
of the child, rather than to produce those results
which nevertheless were produced as the necessary
consequences of my proceedings; and, seeing the
development of different faculties by different
branches of instruction, he came to the conclusion
that the effect of my method was, to lay in the
child a basis of knowledge and of future progress
which must accelerate its education. Krusi saw
that I was no advocate for any hodge-podge of

pedantry ; but that I did with my children what nature does with savages, first ·bringing an image before their eyes, and then seeking a word to express the perception to which it gave rise. He saw that from so simple an acquaintance with the object, no conclusions, no inferences followed ; that there was no doctrine, no point of opinion inculcated, nothing that would *prematurely* excite them to decide between error and truth ; it was a mere matter of intuition, a real basis for conclusions and inferences to be drawn hereafter ; a guide to future discoveries, which, as well as their past experience, they might associate with the substantial knowledge thus acquired.

" He entered more and more into the spirit of my method ; he perceived that success depended upon reducing the different branches of knowledge to their very simplest elements, and proceeding from them in an uninterrupted progress by small and gradual additions. He became every day better fitted to second me in the experiments which I myself made on the ground of the above principles, and, with his assistance, I completed, in a short time, a spelling-book and a course of arithmetic upon my own plan."

Before we proceed to Pestalozzi's other coadjutors, and to the consideration of their opinion of his system, we would draw attention to one important feature in the system. It has been greatly feared that early education has a tendency to injure the brain. We quite agree that premature development often lays the seeds of future disease, but we contend that Pestalozzianism, rightly employed, is diametrically opposed, as we hope we have made evident, to precocious efforts. It never outsteps nature; it seeks not for early blossoms, but watches the powers of the child as they unfold in their natural course; and its aim is to give to each that care and culture which it needs to fit it to perform its proper office. Progressive and harmonious development is its fundamental principle. Thus it first seeks to store the mind intuitively by the operation of the senses —to strengthen the bodily organs by well-graduated exercises—and to cherish the affections of the heart by surrounding the child with an atmosphere of love. This is its first step, and thus it would provide the materials upon which the future education will have to work.* There is only one subject in which the

* A distinguished Professor of Physiology thinks he evinces his skill and prudence by telling us that he does not intend his little boy to learn any lessons till he is eight years old. Pestalozzianism would unite in the cry against early precocity and over-development at any period of youth, but it would have the child learn, as nature evidently designed, long before he is eight; and then nature's lessons, which are the lessons of Pestalozzi, differ altogether from those

child cannot be his own architect; in *religion* he
cannot be too soon taught, that he must receive in

contemplated by the physiologist. They are not tasks set from
books to exercise memory. Pestalozzianism equally agrees with
experience and modern science. A forced development of intelligence in childhood entails either physical feebleness, ultimate
stupidity or early death. The faculties unfold in a given order and
at a given rate. If the course of education conforms itself to that
order and rate, well; if not, if the higher faculties are early taxed by
presenting an order of knowledge more complex and abstract than
can be readily assimilated, or if by excess of culture the intellect is
developed to a degree beyond that which is natural to the age, the
results so produced will inevitably be accompanied by some equivalent, or more than equivalent, evil. Lessons, if given after the
Pestalozzian method, will form a healthful, invigorating, and happy
intellectual and physical exercise, if not a positive recreation.

But there is the cramming system as well as the forcing, and
to it Pestalozzianism is equally opposed. This cramming is a
terrible mistake in every point of view. The mind, like the body,
cannot assimilate beyond a certain rate; and if plied with facts
faster than it can assimilate them, they are very soon rejected.
They do not become permanently built into the intellectual
fabric, but fall out of recollection after the passing of the examination for which they were got up. It is vicious, as tending to
make study distasteful. Either through the painful associations
produced by ceaseless mental toil, or through the abnormal state
of brain it leaves behind, it often generates an aversion to books;
and instead of that subsequent self-culture induced by a rational
education, there comes a continued retrogression. It is a mistake,
inasmuch as it assumes that the acquisition of knowledge is
everything, and forgets that a much more important matter
is the organization or assimiliation of knowledge, for which

faith what he cannot find‘ out for himself. But
even in religious instruction, something may be

time and spontaneous thinking are requisite. Just as Hum-
boldt remarks respecting the progress of intelligence in
general, that "the interpretation of nature is obscured when
the description languishes under too great an accumulation
of insulated facts," so it may be remarked respecting the
progress of individual intelligence, that the mind is overbur-
dened and hampered by an excess of ill-digested information.
Cramming is fatal to that bodily or animal vigour which is
needful to make intellectual training available in the struggle of
life. Success in the world depends much more on energy than
information, and the policy which undermines energy is self-
defeating. The strong will and untiring activity which result from
abundant animal vigour go far to compensate for even great defects
of education ; and when joined with that adequate education
which can be obtained without injuring health, they ensure an easy
victory over competitors enfeebled by excessive study. A comparatively small engine worked at high pressure will do more than
a larger and well-finished one at low pressure. What folly it is,
then, while finishing the engine, so to damage the boiler that it will
not generate steam.

The effect of a forcing system on girls is, if possible, more
injurious than on boys. Being in a great measure debarred from
those vigorous and enjoyable exercises of body by which boys
mitigate the evils of excessive study, girls feel these evils in their
full intensity. Hence the much smaller proportion of them that
grow up well-made and healthy. In pale, angular, flat-chested
young women we see the effects of merciless application, unrelieved
by youthful sports. And this physical degeneracy hinders their
welfare far more than accomplishments aid it. Mothers anxious to
make their daughters attractive could scarcely choose a course

found in the child himself, analogous to the truth to be communicated, and to which it may be linked. We cannot err in this, for our great Teacher led His learners from what they knew and saw to what was spiritual and invisible.*

more fatal than this, which sacrifices the body to the mind. Physical beauty, good-nature, and sound sense will attract more than learning and the blue-stocking. In every point of view the forcing system of education should be eschewed with respect to girls. If there is to be "a coming race," women members of colleges, possessed alike of mental power and acquirement, it will not be in connection with stunted bodily forms, feebleness, and ill-health ; but the product of a progressive, entire, and harmonious development of the elements of human nature. With unmixed satisfaction every Educationist must hail the growing attention paid to physical exercises in our schools, and endeavour to promote it until the intellectual and the physical shall be so balanced that we shall have not in sentiment, but in fact, "a sound mind in a sound body."

* In thus pointing out that religious knowledge is not matter of discovery by the child, but of communication by the teacher, Miss Mayo utters no uncertain sound, and at the same time shows that the educational principles of Pestalozzi may be grafted on and carried out with the soundest evangelical views. Whilst Pestalozzi disapproved of the attempts of Educationists to draw forth from the minds of children intellectual ideas before they had stores of knowledge, he seemed to forget the application of his own principle to moral subjects, or to imagine that this most elevated species of knowledge was innate. In accordance with the delusion that man possesses a general "verifying faculty," Pestalozzi attempted to draw from the minds of his pupils those great truths of religion and the spiritual world which can only be acquired from revelation ; and

Another of those devoted men who joined Pestalozzi in his great work, and shared with him his disappointments and his hopes, his sorrows and his
joys, his obloquy and his fame, was Tobler. He,
like Krusi, had been engaged in education, and,
like him, was dissatisfied with his own labours and

thus led them to imagine that they were competent to judge on this
subject without external aid. Such a course would fall in unhappily
with the tendency produced by other parts of the plan, and we
could not hope to educate in such a mode a truly Christian community. Above all, it is to be regretted (and our teachers are to be
warned against it), that, in reference to religious education, he fell
nto an important error of his predecessors. His too exclusive
attention to mathematical and scientific subjects tended, like the
system of Basedow, to give his pupils the habit of undervaluing historical evidence and of demanding rational demonstration for every
truth, or of requiring the evidence of their senses, to which they
were constantly called to appeal in their studies of natural history.
It is precisely in this way that many men of profound scientific
attainments have been led to reject the evidence of revelation,
and some even, strange as it may seem, to deny the existence
of Him whose works and laws they study. In some of the
early Pestalozzian schools feelings of this nature were particularly
cherished by the habit of asserting a falsehood in the lessons on
mathematics or natural history, and calling upon the pupils to
contradict it, or disprove it, if they did not admit its truth. No
improvement of the intellectual powers can, in our view, compensate for the injury to the moral sense, and the diminished respect
for truth, which will naturally result from such a course, although it
may be quite unintentionally adopted, and with no hostility to the
Bible or its holy truths.

amount of success, his knowledge of the science not being sufficient to enable him to attain to his ideal standard of excellence. Such a state of mind is, however, very favourable to the growth of that humility and teachableness which prepares us for the reception of new truths. Tobler had a considerable share of miscellaneous and superficial knowledge, but he knew little or nothing of the principles of education, and he describes, in a lively manner, the bitter disappointment he experienced on finding the results he obtained from his pupils so very inadequate to the zeal and exertion he bestowed upon them. He had dealt with books, and had found that the language in which they were written was above the comprehension of his learners, and the ideas beyond the sphere of their experience. He next tried Socratic conversations, and endeavoured, by questions and explanations, to bring his pupils to the point he desired; but again he was foiled. How, indeed, could the explanation of words by words, to which no real knowledge corresponded in the mind of the pupil, enlighten and fix itself in the understanding? He was grieved to find that what his children seemed to comprehend one day would, in a few days after, have vanished from their recollection. The more he worked, the less satisfactory

was the progress of his children. While thus groping after his *beau ideal* of instruction, and conscious that he was not even on the road to reach it,
Pestalozzi and his system were brought to his notice,
and when a proposition was made to him of co-
operating, he responded at once to the invitation.
On visiting the school at Bergdorf, he immediately
saw that Pestalozzi arrived by the most simple
means at the ends he had in vain been seeking—
by means, indeed, so simple, that he could not but
marvel that he had not himself made use of them.
He was struck by finding that his discoveries were
of the kind that might be called obvious and simple;
yet the intellectual power and energy manifested
by the pupils proved that their exercises were calculated to develop their faculties. There were some
things to which he could not altogether give his
approbation; indeed, Pestalozzi did not always
adhere to his own grand and fundamental principles; he was yet feeling his way and working
out his own conceptions. An instance of what
must be considered erroneous teaching was the
dictation of difficult and complicated propositions,
which could only at first make a very confused
impression upon his pupils. Pestalozzi's vindication of this exercise was, that Nature herself presents all kinds of things to our view in obscurity

and confusion, but that nevertheless she gradually but certainly conducts into light. Dr. Biber remarks upon this : — " That the preceptions which nature presents, however confused or otherwise obscure they may be, are realities, and therefore contain in themselves the very elements of clearness, and, at the same time, a very strong inducement to search for those elements. But confused impressions made upon us by words are not realities, but mere shadows ; they have in themselves the elements of confusion ; they neither offer an inducement, nor afford the means for clearing them up. The former call out the mind, the latter cramp it. The very power that Pestalozzi possessed over his pupils—to what was it owing (according to the statements both of himself and his friends), but to his making a rule of supplying the child with a clear and distinct notion of the reality before he gave it the sign or shadow — the name ? He declares himself that it was the characteristic feature of his method of teaching language, that he reduced it to the utmost simplicity by excluding from it every combination of words which presupposes a knowledge of language. He was not, however, at all times equally clear on this point, although it lies at the very foundation of many improvements which he made in elementary instruction ; and the

darkness in which it occasionally presented itself to
his mind is, more than anything we could say, calculated to vindicate him against the imputation of
being a mere theorist; his theory throughout was
the fruit of practice, his philosophy of the human
mind essentially experimental."

To return to Tobler. It soon became evident to
him that Pestalozzi attached but little importance
to the separate details of his experiment. Many
exercises were rejected after trial, or when they
had answered his purpose of stimulating the internal power of his children, or of giving to himself
a deeper insight into the principles upon which he
based his experiments. Tobler says :—" I gradually
saw that Pestalozzi's modes of instruction, though
ever varied in detail, had a connection running
through them which made each instrumental in
forwarding the success of the whole, and principally
in effecting the development in the children of the
power of progressing simultaneously in all. Pestalozzi never relaxed his efforts to mature his
plans, till he considered it physically impossible to
proceed further in simplifying them."

Tobler soon arrived at the conviction—a conviction, indeed, which he was prepared to receive from
his own want of success—that all attempts to develop
the mind by means of complicated and artificial

language have in themselves the principles of failure; and that, in order to work with nature, and aid her in her spontaneous development, there must be the utmost simplicity in all instruction, both in the construction of the exercise and in the language used.

"I then," he adds, "began by degrees to perceive why Pestalozzi set aside, *at first*, the abstract rules of grammar; and why his aim was to bring the child to an intuitive perception of number, aiming thus to produce in him a clear and indelible impression that all arithmetic is nothing but an abridgment of the simple process of numeration, and the numbers themselves an abridgment of the wearisome repetition of one, and one, and one, make, &c. Also, why he considered an aptitude in the art of drawing lines, angles, curves, &c., to be the basis of all aptitude for the arts, and of representing objects either seen or conceived. My conviction of the advantages of his system strengthened every day, as I witnessed the general development of the power of measuring, calculating, writing, and drawing."

Tobler also heartily concurred in the paramount desire of Pestalozzi—that of enabling parents to become the teachers of their children by simplifying for them all instruction and furnishing them with a practical method of universal application. *

* It has been considered an error in the system of Pestalozzi that he simplified too much, although we see that simplification and thoroughness in teaching elements were the points that excited the admiration and convinced the judgment of Tobler respecting the excellence of these methods, and secured his adhesion to the cause. Woodbridge says :—"Simplification was carried too far and continued too long. The mind became so accustomed to receive knowledge divided into its most simple elements, that it was not prepared to embrace complicated ideas, or to make those rapid strides in investigation and conclusion which is one of the most important results of a sound education, and indicates the most valuable kind of mental vigour both for scientific purposes and practical life." This is a heavy charge, both as to the defective method and its consequences. Occasionally there may have been abuse of this excellent principle, but as an habitual practice it could not have been so, whether we take Woodbridge's own admission, the testimony of others respecting the intellectual vigour and acuteness of the pupils at Yverdon, or other leading principles of the system. Whilst Pestalozzi held the necessity of simplification, he was equally clear on instruction being adapted to the attainments, the capacity, and the power of children. The mottoes of the school have ever been—"Milk for babes, strong meat for the full-grown." "It is doubtful which is the greater evil, that the instruction should be above or below the children." "The child should not be fitted for the instruction, but the instruction for the child," because "instruction is the means, the improvement of the child the end, of education." "Deal with children as you find them, intellectually as well as morally." Simplification with Pestalozzi generally meant what the word literally means, reduction to elements, and could only be misapplied where the age and capacity of the children fitted them for what was abstract and complicated. It is, however, a

We now leave Tobler, to speak of a third co-adjutor of Pestalozzi—Buss. Though born in the lower ranks of life, his parents had intended to qualify him for a literary career. He had early shown talent and an aptitude for learning. At twelve years old he had fitted himself to teach music and drawing, and had applied himself with industry to the study of the ancient languages, rhetoric, and logic; but depressed by the hand of poverty, and overpowered by difficulties that frustrated all his hopes of advancement, he was almost brought to the brink of despair, when it was proposed to him to become a teacher of music and drawing in the establishment of Pestalozzi at Bergdorf. His necessity, rather than his inclination, impelled him to accede to the proposal, for he had heard of Pestalozzi only as a wild enthusiast, whose schemes were visionary and impracticable. He gives the following account of his first impressions :—

"On entering the school, I saw nothing in it but confusion, and what appeared to me an un-

point on which young teachers should be very careful, whether for their own character as to skill and consistency, the progress of their children, or the criticisms of Inspectors, who very properly object to "thin lessons." The elements into which Pestalozzi reduced instruction will be found farther on in this volume.

comfortable bustle. But my interest had been so
excited the day before by the strong eulogium I
had heard of Pestalozzi's plan, that I struggled against
my own impressions, and soon began to appreciate
his method of teaching. At first I thought that
the children were detained too long at one point,
but when I observedthe perfection they attained
in their elementary exercises, I was convinced that
the failure of my own education arose from its
incoherent and desultory character. I now clearly
saw that had I applied in my boyhood with equal
energy to first elements, I should by this time have
acquired a mental independence, and not have had
the same distressing difficulties to struggle against.
I learnt the power of one of Pestalozzi's principles,
that, by his method, men are to be rendered capable
of helping themselves ; and it is my own experience
that no one can help the man that cannot help
himself.

" I directed my attention principally to that
branch of instruction in which my services were
required, but it was long before I understood what
were the peculiar views which Pestalozzi held with
regard to drawing. I could not tell what he meant
when he affirmed that lines, angles, and curves are
the basis of drawing. By degrees I arrived at the
conviction that I must set aside my own previous

knowledge, and descend to the simple elements, in the application of which I saw his strength consisted; though, as yet, I could not altogether follow him. However, the observation of the progress made by the children in dwelling perseveringly on the elements of knowledge at last brought conviction and clearness to my own mind, and, relinquishing my former ideas, I was enabled in a few days to draw up my sketch of an alphabet of form according to Pestalozzi's ideas.

"I now fell into another error. As hitherto I had never separated in my imagination the outline from the object, so now I saw nothing but lines; and I imagined that children must be exercised on these lines exclusively, in every branch of drawing, before real objects were to be placed before them for imitation or even for comparison. Pestalozzi, on the contrary, considered his lessons on drawing in connection with the whole of his system, and with nature, which never leaves any branch of art to remain isolated in the mind. He proposed to draw out a plan of teaching in which it was his intention to lay before the child two distinct series of figures. By the first he desired to lead him to an intuitive knowledge of things, and by the other to furnish practical illustrations for a course of lessons on abstract forms."

This alphabet of forms to which Buss alludes was one of the plans which were superseded by more matured judgment. Buss was very much struck with one of the essential objects of Pestalozzi's method, which was, always to connect language with the knowledge gained from nature by the help of art: at every stage of instruction the pupil was to be supplied with appropriate expressions for what he learned. Though Buss judged of the system at first in its application to drawing, he made himself acquainted also with its bearing upon other branches of instruction. He observes :—

"I saw that as it was possible to proceed from lines to angles, from angles to figures, and from figures to real objects, in the art of drawing, so likewise in language, we can proceed from sounds to words, and from words to sentences, and thereby bring the child to equal clearness on that subject. I saw the same principle carried out in arithmetic. I had before regarded numbers without a clear notion of the value or contents of each ; I acquired now a distinct and intuitive idea of the extent of each number, and this I found. was the secret of the pupil's success." He concludes his narrative with the following grateful testimony :—

"One word more I add. My acquaintance with Pestalozzi's method has, in a great measure, restored to me the cheerfulness and energy of my younger days, and has rekindled in my breast those hopes of improvement for myself and my species which I had for a long time esteemed as vain dreams, and had cast away, contrary to the dictates of my heart."

Besides the three valuable assistants we have mentioned, many more were attracted to Pestalozzi's side by the increasing interest his system excited. Amongst the number was a young minister of the name of Niederer, who, equally struck with the value of the system and the greatness of the object Pestalozzi had in view, devoted himself to his service with the utmost zeal and energy. The vigorous mind of Pestalozzi laboured with ideas that he had not the power of communicating with clearness to others, probably, in part, because they were not clearly defined to himself. Niederer united to expansion of mind and power of abstraction a clearness, precision, and accuracy, which made his co-operation peculiarly valuable. He was enabled to disentangle and arrange much that was involved and perplexed, and to clear up and render practical much that was obscure and metaphysical. He regarded the work as a noble work; and he loved the simple-hearted philosopher, who, with such complete self-abandonment, could toil on, in

spite of difficulties, discouragement, and contempt,
for the amelioration of the rising generation.*
With the help of this phalanx of talented men
the Institution at Bergdorf was brought into a
complete state of organization. The desultory
teaching and the experimental and ever-varying
lessons were superseded by regular courses of in-

* Another of the coadjutors of Pestalozzi, though never at
Yverdon, was Hans Georg Nägeli, by whose compositions and
teaching the Pestalozzian method of instruction was applied to the
study of music. After receiving his rudimentary education at home,
and perfecting it at Zürich, he devoted himself carefully to the study
of music. He became a composer and publisher of music, and in
1800 established a periodical principally devoted to his favourite
art. His song, "Life let us cherish," with accompaniments of harp
and harpsichord, published in 1794, was welcomed at the fireside
and the social gatherings of rich and poor all over Europe. In 1810
he published in connection with M. S. Pfeiffer, who had passed
some time in the establishment at Yverdon, "The Theory of
Instruction in Singing on Pestalozzian Principles," by which a new
epoch in the department of education was introduced. The
treatise, which consisted of a well-graduated series of exercises,
was the best realization of the method of Pestalozzi. He soon
made singing a regular study in the popular schools of Europe,
particularly in those of Switzerland and Germany. By the
efforts of William C. Woodbridge and Lowell Mason, the
method of Nägeli was introduced into the United States.
The latter made an effort at the Home and Colonial School
Society many years ago to introduce it into our English schools,
but no one came forward with sufficient spirit and intelligence to
take it up.

struction, which, after their value had been tested
in the schoolroom, were collected and published
in six parts in 1803, under the title of "Pestalozzi's
Elementary Books." They comprised a manual of
arithmetic, one of elementary geometry, and one of
language, in accordance with the three elements
into which Pestalozzi reduced instruction. Their
separate titles were, "Intuitive Instruction in the
Proportions of Numbers. Two Parts,"— and
"The Mother's Manual; or, Help to Mothers in
Teaching their Children the Art of Observing and
Speaking. One Part." Pestalozzi was much disappointed in the little success that attended these
works. Their failure is, perhaps, more to be attributed to the want of preparedness in the public
mind for this advance in education, than to
defects in the works; though, it must be confessed,
there is much in them that is crude, much that is
minute to weariness, much that plain sense would
reject as visionary. Exercises, worked out by those
who were imbued with the spirit of the author,
and whose enthusiasm itself almost ensured success,
appeared altogether different when clothed in imperfect language, and presented as a dead letter instead
of a living sound.*

* We are now placed beyond the region of experiment.
The admirable manuals on Number and Form, by Mr. Reiner,

K 2

We have been tempted to give this account of the men whom Pestalozzi drew around him, and of their efforts, because they are the best expositors of his views on education, to unfold which is our primary object. But we now turn to Pestalozzi himself. It is interesting, as we trace his life, to mark the singular contrarieties which distinguish it The man himself, we see, was remarkable for his tenacity of purpose, for the strength and steadiness of his convictions. His outward lot, however, was a very chequered and trying one; the vicissitudes which he was called to encounter were sufficient to have daunted a less resolute, as they would certainly have chilled a less benevolent, mind. Pestalozzi, however, was steady to his purpose, and, under all changes, true to his fundamental principles. We shall again see this exemplified as we proceed to sketch the close of his career.

At Bergdorf, as we have related, his plans were rapidly maturing, and his well-earned celebrity was drawing around him a class of disciples who were

present us with a series of exercises that only need the intelligence and energy of the living teacher to give them power. The elementary Lessons on Language given in our Infant School Manual form a safe guide, as far as they go, and we have numerous specimens of lessons on other subjects in the various works published by the Society.

fully prepared to share in his sufferings and his toils. The fruit of his labours, too, was now visible, not only in his school, but, to some degree, in his published works. The latter, however, did not become a source of pecuniary profit, nor afford him the help he needed for the support of his Institution. Added to this, a new revolution of the political wheel deprived him of the help which hitherto he had received from the Helvetic Government, and thus his prospects were again clouded. In this emergency, however, the Government of the Canton de Vaud invited him to transfer his establishment to their territory, giving him the choice of several castles which were now left vacant by the retiring Deputies. It happened at the same time that he received another offer from Emmanuel de Fellenberg, well known for his zealous efforts in the cause of education. Fellenberg proposed that he should establish himself on an estate of his own at Munchen Buchsee, and there were many reasons which might have induced Pestalozzi to close with the proposal, especially the prospect of being associated with a kindred spirit, and a man occupying so influential a position in society. Circumstances like these promised great help to our philanthropist; but, on the other hand, he feared that, while securing a powerful friend, he might also find himself shackled in carrying out his system, owing to the different views entertained by Fellenberg and himself on the subject of education; and thus he might be placed in a very invidious position with reference to his benevolent patron. There was much which the two held in common; on the other hand, there were some fundamental points on which they differed. It was Fellenberg's object to fit the child for his particular position in society—to educate him for the world. Pestalozzi took a higher view, and contended that the educator ought to regard the child, not with reference to the artificial institutions of society, but with a view to what he is in himself. He desired to consider for what God had destined him, and to educate the child in accordance with the will and purpose of his heavenly Father; and certainly, into whatever mistakes his followers may since have fallen, it must, we think, be admitted that this principle—the very basis of Pestalozzianism—is precisely that which best harmonizes with our holy religion.

In deciding upon the future locality of his labours, Pestalozzi took a middle course; he sent the poor children to Munchen Buchsee (where, however, they did not long remain), and established himself, with his pupils of the middle and higher classes, at the Castle of Yverdon, a situation of great beauty, on the southern side of the lake of Neuchâtel.

In his expansive benevolence, Pestalozzi had contemplated both an orphan asylum and a school for
training teachers ; but the want of sufficient funds
obliged him to abandon the idea of separate establishments for these purposes, and he could only
carry out his intentions to a limited extent, by
admitting to his school young men of small means,
chiefly from the middle class, whose desire was to
devote themselves to the work of education. Many
of these subsequently became valuable teachers, and
were instrumental in disseminating his principles
very widely through various parts of the Continent.*

* Although Pestalozzi did not reach the object of his ambition, in
having a formal Training Institution, yet he trained his teachers in
the most practical of all ways, and one which it is heartily to be
desired that school-masters and mistresses would adopt in the
training of their pupil-teachers. Dr. Biber tells us in his "Life of
Pestalozzi," that :—" In the training and superintendence of his
teachers, more was required than formal and didactic instruction in
method, the appointment of certain duties, and the promise of a
certain salary. He awakened in them a deep sense of the exalted
and responsible character of their office, and gave persevering
encouragement to their zeal. For this purpose, Pestalozzi endeavoured to make the teaching of others a source of instruction,
the government of others a means of moral improvement to themselves. On two evenings in the week he met all the teachers in a
general assembly, alternately devoted to the discussion of the general
means of instruction and discipline, and of the individual state of
each pupil. Every teacher in his turn was called upon to give an
account of the manner in which he proceeded in his lessons, and of

It is difficult to estimate the impetus thus given to the cause he loved, and the extent of the influence which Pestalozzi himself thus acquired. His fame in Germany, Prussia, and Russia was now high; and the Emperor Alexander, to mark his sense of the benefit conferred upon the latter country by the education of some of its young Princes, and the supply of a body of able teachers, conferred upon him the decoration of one of the Russian orders. Pestalozzi, indeed, seemed now to have reached the

the children who were placed under his instruction or superintendence. He was encouraged in communicating his observations, stating his difficulties, and offering suggestions; he had to expect from Pestalozzi and from his brother teachers nothing but cordial assent where he was in the right, and kind advice or gentle reproof where he was in the wrong. In these assemblies the younger teachers learned, by the manner in which they were treated by the elder members of the establishment, the difficult art of living on an equality with those who were in a certain sense their inferiors, without descending to a level with them. The remarks of each, together with the resolutions to which they led, were put down in a minute-book, which, while it formed the basis of candid correspondence with the parents, served as a useful reference for any teacher who might wish for information on some particular branch of the method, or concerning some one or other of the pupils. The effect of these constant communications on every subject connected with their daily duties could not fail to produce unity of feeling, of thought, and action among all the teachers of the establishment. They were not left to first impressions and prejudiced views; they could not for any length of time overrate or underrate the abilities, acquirements,

zenith of his fame. Pupils of all countries and of
all ranks flocked to his school. And truly he
presided there as the father of a family, diffusing
around him an atmosphere of harmony and love;
while, at the same time, he inspired his pupils with
an energy, an *esprit de corps*, and a confidence of
success, which, under his fostering care, enabled them
to accomplish wonders.

The following sketch by Dr. Biber will fully
verify what we have said of the spirit which reigned

or moral deserts of any of the children. The experience of one man
threw light upon that of another; one trait, one fact, explained
another; and much of the injustice of which a single teacher will
often become guilty was prevented by the full picture which was
drawn by all in common of the state of mind of each pupil; not to
mention the rich store of general knowledge of human nature which
these conversations must have been the means of eliciting from, and
impressing upon, the minds of all present.

"Another assembly of the teachers took place on Saturday evenings, for the purpose of collecting whatever observations might have
been made by each during the course of the week on matters of
general discipline, order, &c. Defects in the management, incon-
veniences in the arrangement of the house, mistakes on the part of
teachers, and misdemeanours on the part of pupils were here
brought under discussion. The result of these deliberations, likewise, was put on record.

"In a general assembly of teachers and pupils, held on Sunday
evenings, such points as referred to the conduct of the latter were
introduced, and their attention directed towards the means of
remedying existing evils, or of attaining any object that was found
desirable in a moral or religious point of view."

in Pestalozzi's establishment. ' Writing as an eye-
witness, he says :—

" Never, perhaps, has the idea of domestic life,
in the highest sense of the word, 'been more beautifully realized, never the effect of a Christian family
spirit more powerfully illustrated, than in the
flourishing times of the establishment at Yverdon,
in which persons of all ages, of all ranks, of all
nations, persons of the most different gifts and
abilities, and of the most opposite characters, were
united together by that unaffected love which
Pestalozzi, in years a man verging to the grave, but
in heart and mind a genuine child, seemed to
breathe out continually, and to impart to all that
came within his circle. His children forgot that
they had any other home, his teachers that
there was any other world besides the Institution.
Even the oldest members of this great family, men
who had attained all the maturity of manhood,
venerated Pestalozzi with all the reverence of true filial
affection, and cherished towards each other, and
towards the younger teachers and pupils, a genuine
brotherly feeling such as has, perhaps, never existed on
earth since the days of the pristine Christian Church.
The children saw in Pestalozzi their father, in the
teachers of the house their elder brethren ; and
they needed no rules to keep them in subjection

where a constant exercise of kindness imposed on them the restraint of duty and hourly obligation." *

The most imperfect part of the undertaking was perhaps that to which the public attention has been chiefly directed, and which has been most vaunted,

---

* " To awaken that feeling in the children required on the part of the teachers a greater self-denial than most heads of establishments would find it possible to impose on their assistants. But Pestalozzi's example operated like a spell; and his teachers submitted in his house to arrangements which the same men, perhaps, would nowhere else have been able to endure. They had the immediate inspection of the different apartments, as well as of the books of the children. In the morning every teacher assisted those that were especially committed to his care in washing and dressing themselves; which being done, he conducted them to the great hall, where the whole family were assembled for morning service. During the day he lost sight of them only while they were engaged in lessons with other teachers ; but at meals, and in the hours of recreation, he joined them again ; he participated in their play, accompanied them in their walks, and at the close of the day followed them again to evening prayers, and thence to bed. Yet in all this there was on the part of the pupils perfect freedom ; they were not forced to be with their teacher, but their teacher was always ready to be with them ; and as his presence imposed on them no artificial restraint, they delighted in his company. They found his conversation entertaining, his advice encouraging ; their games became more interesting by his participation, their walks more instructive by the information they derived from him, and their conscience was strengthened by the glance of his eye."—*Biber.*

viz., the new method of instruction. The spirit
which pervaded the whole, and which constituted
the vital principle of Pestalozzi's education, was less
tangible than a set of printed lesson tables; and
hence it is that travellers, inquirers, and observers,
from near and far, while they have hardly caught a
glimpse of the former, have inundated the world
with fragments of the latter, which could not but
prove inefficient and worthless, like to a branch
which must necessarily wither when it is cut from
the tree on which it grew. Much of the reproach
which has been heaped upon the cause is to be
attributed to this circumstance. The disproportion
between the effects announced, and the results
actually obtained by men who converted the means
engrafted upon the life of the Institution at
Yverdon into a dead system, and transferred them
on a dead ground, has also prejudiced many even
against those branches of the method which Pestalozzi and his teachers had succeeded in establishing.
Moreover, the imperfect state in which they themselves left some departments of instruction furnished
an additional argument against them with the large
mass of the public, who care not whether their
judgment be fair or unfair, provided they can
support it by facts.

It was not, indeed, to be expected that a discovery which tended to a universal reform of all human knowledge, not merely in the manner of conveying it, but in the basis on which it is to be founded, and the purpose for which it is to be imparted, should be practically applied to the whole range of science by one man who, at the time when he engaged in the work, had attained an age at which most men retire from every active pursuit. If those who are unable to comprehend, or unwilling to acknowledge whatever is more lofty or ˙more enlarged than the commonplace chronicle of their own consciousness, must needs have something to be surprised at, let them wonder that Pestalozzi realized so much of his views rather than that he did not realize them all. What he did was a seed of truth sown on the field of human culture, and though much of it may have fallen by the wayside, and on stony places, and among thorns, yet some of it will bring forth fruit an hundredfold.

We will now quote the testimony of one who loved Pestalozzi as a father, and was himself loved as a son, while, at the same time, he was regarded with a peculiar interest as one sent to cheer his latter days and revive the hope which our philanthropist had long and ardently cherished, that his system would at length be introduced into England, and there be duly understood and appreciated. The

Rev. Dr. Mayo, to whom we here allude, was persuaded by some friends, in the year 1818, to take
charge of a party of English youths who were sent
to Yverdon for education. Whilst he acted as their
chaplain, and was, in some degree, responsible to
their parents for their education, he took advantage
of the opportunity to make himself acquainted with
a system which was exciting the most wide-spread
interest, and, in fact, re-modelling education on the
Continent. At first he saw but little to admire;
there was much which did not at once commend it
to an Englishman and a classical scholar. Its
principles lay deep, and were often obscured by the
manner in which they were carried out. But
gradually he perceived the beauty and value of the
"idea of the system," and separated it from "the
form," which would vary in different hands, and
might be accommodated to different circumstances;
he caught the enthusiasm that reigned at the Institution, and hoped that, by transplanting the system
to his own country, he might bestow upon it an
invaluable boon. With this conviction, he was
content to forego a career of distinction which might
have been open to him in his own country, and,
imitating his teacher in self-abandonment, he
returned to England, determined to fulfil the
arduous but little estimated labours of a school-

master, and to give a practical exhibition of the system of Pestalozzi, modified however, and adapted to the English mind and character. With these views, he opened a school for the education of the higher classes at Cheam, in Surrey. The success which attended his exertions is well-known, and need not be described.* His account of the impression made upon him by Pestalozzi and his work may be seen in the Memoir already given.

---

* From the Cheam School emanated those little treatises on elementary instruction which are alike monuments of practical skill and illustrations of the methods of Pestalozzi.—"Lessons on Objects," "Lessons on Shells," "Lessons on Number," "Lessons on Form," and "The Cheam Latin Grammar," with introductions by Dr. Mayo, expounding the principles on which the lessons were drawn up. Although we have no record of the particular modes of working the Cheam School, yet from the subjoined hymns which were sung there we may gather something of the spirit that was cultivated. The sentiments breathed in these hymns are those of true religion: a religion that recognizes God as our gracious Father, through the Lord Jesus Christ, as our Atoning Saviour and elder Brother; God in providence, God in daily life; earth as our place of probation and sphere of holiness, with heaven as our home; the brotherhood of humanity and especially of Christians, in all its loving sympathy and interest. It must have been delightful to hear many scores of young hearts sending forth these strains of piety and love.

I.—MORNING HYMN.

(Sung at Cheam School.)

FROM danger through the night
Thou, Lord, hast kept me free :
The darkness and the light
Are both alike to Thee.

A prayerful spirit, Lord,
A watchful frame impart ;
Teach me to love Thy Word,
And hide it in my heart.

My daily wants supply,
Preserve my life from harm,
And guide me with Thine eye,
And guard me with Thine arm.

My studious toil employ
Its portions of the day ;
And sinless be the joy
That animates my play.

May I each moment hear
My Father's warning voice ;
And know that Thou art near,
And, knowing it, rejoice.

May grace my heart incline
To walk in all Thy ways ;
The blessing, Lord, be mine,
And Thine be all the praise.

II.—THE WELCOME.

(Sung at Cheam School at the entrance of a Pupil.)

WELCOME, brother ! welcome here ;
Banish every doubt and fear.
No unkindness would agree
With a Christian family.
Ev'ry heart will hold thee dear—
Welcome, brother ! welcome here.

We have wept as well as you ;
We have left our parents too ;
But we've found—and you will find—
Friends affectionate and kind.
Let us, then, your spirits cheer
With our welcome, brother, here.

Here our time we gaily spend,
Work and play together blend ;
Changing studies wing the hours,
Many a cheerful sport is ours ;
Seldom drops the bitter tear—
Welcome, brother ! welcome here.

Brother, wilt thou learn to prize
Jesu's spotless sacrifice ?
Wilt thou learn to walk with Him
Tow'rd the " New Jerusalem ? "
Wilt thou Jesu's name revere?
Welcome, brother ! welcome here.

Here, a little band, we raise
Songs of joy and hymns of praise,
May we all in realms above
Sing of Jesu's dying love ;
While resounds the starry sphere,
Welcome, brother ! welcome here.

III.—THE FAREWELL.

(Sung at Cheam School at the departure of a Pupil.)

FARE thee well ! and yet bethink thee
   Of the bands by friendship twin'd ;
Let remembrance firmly link thee
   To companions left behind.

Fare thee well ! may heaven's protection
   Guard thy op'ning life's career ;
So each snare shall meet detection,
   So each danger disappear.

May thy cup o'erflow with gladness,
   Rich in proofs of Jesu's love ;
And each passing hour of sadness
   Point thy views to joys above.

Years of blessing may'st thou number,
   Not one moment spent in vain ;
May'st thou then in Jesus slumber,
   And in Jesus rise again.

To our Father's house invited,
   May we all His praises swell ;
And in love and joy united,
   Hear no more the word—Farewell !

Pestalozzi terminated his mortal career whilst on a visit to Brugg, Feb. 17, 1827, aged eighty-one. We desire to draw a veil over his declining years, content to admire the general tenor of his course, through a long life, and to hold him up as one of the greatest benefactors whom God has raised up

to bless mankind. It would require no common pen
to do justice to the character of "Father Pestalozzi;"
so rare a combination of gigantic powers and childlike simplicity — such unconquerable energy and
vigour, yet such tender love—such profuse generosity, yet such frugal habits—such active zeal, yet
such unwavering perseverance. His religion has
been attacked, and we will not deny that some
degree of vagueness and uncertainty may have
obscured his views; but it is evident he had imbibed
the spirit of the meek and lowly Jesus, and that the
Bible was the acknowledged guide by which he
desired to mould his conduct.

THE PRINCIPLES OF PESTALOZZI.*

We must hasten, however, to our second point,
which is to show what are the principles of Pesta-

* In the text the principles of Pestalozzi are stated rather
as rules than principles. Principles are facts or reasons; rules
are practical. The former are found in the nature of the children,
and lie deeper than rules. In fact, the rules are based on application of the principles, being the practical conclusions drawn from
them. Dr. Mayo's first principle, that education should be
essentially religious, would be more fully stated thus—that man
being a moral and religious creature, and religion (*religere*, to bind
again, or fast) being the appointed means of binding man to man,
and rebinding him to his God, from whom he has broken off,
education should be essentially moral and religious.

lozzi, or, in other words, in what his system essentially consists; and to do this we shall avail ourselves largely of what has been written by others. Our first extract is from a short Memoir of Pestalozzi appended to some letters of his written to a Mr. Greaves. It may be regarded as giving us the first great fundamental principles of his system. Pestalozzi, the Memoir states, maintains that every plan of education ought to be based on a consideration of the nature of the child, and that in developing the faculties (which is the business of education) it should be remembered that their germs are in existence in the child, and that only when brought into play in their natural connection with each other do they form, as they ought to do, *an organic whole ;* that in every individual they appear under certain modifications, which render it necessary that the strictest attention should be paid to the *shades of individual character and talent ;* that in different stages of development they require a *different and seasonable treatment ;* that which is commonly called instruction is no more than the *means employed to develop and exercise these faculties*, and that these means ought to *keep pace with the state of the faculties* which they are designed to exercise.

" It is obvious that the subject to commence with should be no other than the child himself ; and first

of all, his physical nature, namely, the principal parts
of the body, the limbs and the senses, with their
corresponding organs; and while the names are
supplied and the attention is thus drawn towards
the former, exercises ought to accompany the knowledge, to give it at once a practical character, thus
rendering the senses active and alert, accustoming
the eye to distinguish colours, and the ear sounds, &c.,
and to strengthen and diversify the different movements of the body. This introduces infant gymnas-
tics. The senses, of course, as the connecting
medium, lead to a consideration of the material
world, beginning by that which is nearest and
stands in the most immediate relation to the child.
Here, while language has to furnish the names of
things, observation has to discover their qualities,
and experience, assisted by instruction, to teach
their use and nature. But the material world and
the lessons which it teaches are not to arrest the
attention of the child exclusively; the relation in
which the child stands to those of his own species,
beginning with the first and most endearing—the
family circle— awakens a train of new ideas; feelings which had either been slumbering or acting
only instinctively become objects of consciousness.
With these feelings should be connected an acquaintance with the highest truths and duties, in conformity

with that religious spirit which ought to preside over infant education."

Our second extract is from an English source, and sets forth the principle of *the nature and aim of education*, corroborating the views which Pestalozzi held, so frequently and eloquently advocated, and in his own country and Germany successfully established. The following very just observations, as to what education ought to be, and the extract from Dugald Stewart, with which he supports his enlarged views, are quoted from Mr. Tremenheere, formerly one of H.M.'s Inspectors of Elementary Schools :—

"If the mental and moral condition," Mr. Tremenheere observes, " of the rising generation is to be usefully affected through the medium of schools, wider views must be taken of what it is requisite to teach, and of the instrumentality by which it is to be communicated. It is still necessary to repeat, that what is commonly called education, namely, the teaching the mechanical art of reading and writing, with a little arithmetic, and the dogmatical inculcation of Scripture formularies very imperfectly understood, if at all, is not, in fact, education, or anything more than its unformed, undeveloped germ ; possibly containing within it that which may give some additional power to the mind, but very probably in no way reaching and impressing the heart. It is necessary also to repeat, that if the legitimate educator does no more than this, there are those who will do more—the Chartist and Socialist educator—the publisher of exciting, obscene, and irreligious works—he who can boldly assert and readily declaim upon false and pernicious dogmas and principles. To inculcate the leading doctrines of faith, and to present the main incidents of the Holy Scripture in such a manner as shall interest the affections of the young, and not alone burden the memory, and to impart some real knowledge applicable to the state of society in which they live, and to the world around them—is the work in hand."—*Minutes of Committee*, 1840, p. 437.

Dugald Stewart thus defines the essential objects of education ("Philosophy of the Human Mind," vol. i. p. 20) :—" They are first to cultivate all the various principles of our nature, both speculative and active, in such a manner as to bring them to the greatest perfection of which they are susceptible ; and secondly, by watching over the impressions and associations which the mind receives in early life, to secure it against the influence of prevailing errors, and, so far as possible, to engage in prepossessions on the side of truth. That the teacher may rightly fulfil his duty, in developing and improving the faculties, and in calling forth and regulating the affections of those committed to his charge, it is essential that he should have some acquaintance with the principles of the human mind. In general, his utmost aim at present, corresponding with the extent of his capacity, is to lead the intellect through some of the lower processes of elementary teaching. Even this branch of duty opens to him a field of usefulness, on which he is seldom prepared to enter.

" Again, we should bear in mind that the ultimate end of education is not a perfection in the accomplishments of the school, but *a fitness for life*; not the acquirement of habits of blind obedience and of prescribed diligence, but a preparation for independent action. Whatever class of life a pupil belongs to, whatever calling he may be intended for, there are certain qualities in human nature common to all, which constitute the stock of the fundamental energies of man. We have no right to withhold from any one the opportunities of developing all their faculties. It may be judicious to treat some of them with marked attention, and to give up the idea of bringing others to high perfection. The diversity of talent and inclination, of plans and pursuits, is a sufficient proof of the necessity of such a distinction. But we have no right to shut out the child altogether from the development of those

faculties also which we may not for the present conceive to be essential for his future calling or station
in life. Who is not acquainted with the vicissitudes
of human fortune, which have frequently rendered
attainment valuable that had been little esteemed,
or been led to regret the want of application to an
exercise which had been treated with contempt?"

The principles of Pestalozzi are more fully set forth
in a lecture by the late Rev. Dr. Mayo, delivered at
the Royal Institution, Albermarle Street, in May, 1826.
Of this we avail ourselves.*

* We often hear of the methods of Pestalozzi, many of which
were supposed to have been introduced into this country by Sir. J.
Kay-Shuttleworth and others. The fact is, that Pestalozzi originated
few methods, and those, in general, were not particularly good.
Pestalozzi was not a man of methods, but of principles; and his
system is emphatically one of principles upon which his disciples have
based their methods. None can lay claim to being a Pestalozzian
who is ignorant of the principles of teaching, of government, and of
education. The philosophic mind of Pestalozzi could not be satisfied
with mere methods of instruction, however good. He must needs go
deeper, and discover the principles of school management. To guide
him in teaching, he looked on the one hand at instruction; on the
other, at the nature of the child for whom the instruction was designed.
This led him to make an analysis of the different branches of instruction, teaching these elements one by one before presenting them
in their combined form, as in the usual branches of instruction. It
was in accordance with these principles that the elementary subjects
of Number, Form, Place, &c., &c., were discovered, and introduced
into our infant-schools and nurseries with such success. Pestalozzi

further ascertained whether a subject of instruction was of an inductive or deductive character, and adopted modes of teaching
appropriate to each, reserving the more difficult subject and its
corresponding method for higher stages of development—and he
determined whether the subject was one to be observed in its facts
and reasoned out to its principles, or one to be communicated to the
children.   It was such distinctions which gave rise to the methods
of induction, deduction, and direct communication.   In connection
with the operations of the human mind, Pestalozzi discovered many
of the laws by which these operations are regulated, and finally
concluded that, as to be successful in the material world we must act
in conformity with those physical laws which govern it, so in the
education of children, we must act in conformity with the known
tendencies of their nature.   For his guidance in the discipline and
moral training of children, Pestalozzi contemplated on the one hand
the design of school government and the constituents of *a healthy
moral character*, based on the principles of the Gospel; on the other,
the laws of a child's moral nature, together with the *influence of
intelligence* on the affections and the will.   From these he discovered
the method of obtaining power over children, and the spirit in which
that power should be administered.   Pestalozzi came to the conclusion that the parental spirit must possess the teacher, while kindness,
sympathy, impartiality, and a good example, mingled with judgment
and authority, should be its manifestations.   Pestalozzi would also
add the pastoral to the parental spirit, and lay stress on good
methods of instruction as securing interest and attention, thus
rendering much discipline unnecessary.   When children are kept
busy, he averred, they have no temptation to naughtiness, and the
teacher's duties are light.   For the principles of education, Pestalozzi
looked to the connection between the child's present state and its
future condition and character.   He considered that God had not
only given man a nature, and a sphere of duty in which this nature
was to act; but a destiny to be attained by the workings of character.
It was thus that the system of Pestalozzi was one of principles; and

Principle 1. — *Education should be essentially religious.**—Its end and aim should be to lead a crea-

the methods founded on these are certain, satisfactory, and effective. Pestalozzianism is thoroughly practical, being based on the nature of children and the connection of their present and future states. Moreover, Pestalozzian practice is not mere art, but art supported by science—scientific art.

*This does not mean merely that religion must be taught, but that all things must be taught religiously. Religion is *essential* to education, entering into and pervading school-work, as the essence of anything enters into and pervades that thing. The spirit and power, the principles and motives, if not the words of religion, must be ready to manifest themselves in all parts of school-work, as the blood is in every part of the body, penetrating the whole system, and exhibiting itself at the remotest extremities. Every principle deduced from the sacred volume would then be brought to bear on the ordinary relations, duties, and concerns of the children. The religion of the schoolroom would not be an incidental thing, or one occasionally introduced as a subject of instruction, but the guiding, all-controlling spirit of every action. It would not be merely formal or dogmatic ; but religion in spirit, in aims, in methods, in practice. There would be not only religious lessons and precepts, but religious influence and example. In this pervading and essential character, religion had its place in the school of Pestalozzi. Neither to obviate a religious difficulty, nor to square with the practices of the perfunctory teacher, would Pestalozzi have been satisfied with religious instruction during one hour, banishing all mention of it during the other hours of the day. He pleaded, not indeed for human forms and symbols of faith, as adopted by particular Churches, but for the ubiquity of the religious principle, at all hours and in all doings in the schoolroom. This necessarily implied the presence of the Word of God, and the free inculcation of its truths, precepts, and promises.

ture, born for immortality, to that conformity to the
image of God in which the glory and happiness of

It is striking to notice the thoroughly Christian character of this
principle. The first Churches of Christ did not separate their
religious services from the rest of life, and give them alone the name
of worship. To them, as the heritage of the Lord, the whole of life
was worship, and every act sanctified by the Holy Ghost an accept-
able service. Hence the terms, "worship," "service," "sacrifice"
are never in the New Testament applied exclusively to acts of
devotion, whether public or private, but embrace the whole life.
"Present your bodies (or your bodily actions) a living sacrifice
. . . . which is your reasonable service." "Pure religion (worship)
and undefiled . . . . is to visit the fatherless and widows in their
affliction, and to keep himself unspotted (in the transactions of life)
from the world." "Do good and communicate . . . . for with such
sacrifices God is well pleased."

The pervading character of religion in true education is well
illustrated in the practice of the Abbé Girard. Whilst his chief
subject in school was language, the truths of morality and religion
were so blended with other instruction that his pupils received them
almost unawares. His anecdote of a visitor sets this in a striking
light. "In 1820, one of the secular clergy, a teacher at Genoa,
was sent by his superior to Switzerland, to visit schools and borrow
from them a better system than was then practised in Italy. He
remained for some weeks in my school, during which time we had
very little conversation. He was busy collecting his facts, and I was
well content he should do so. When he had completed his observations, he came to me and said, 'I have discovered the secret of your
method. Your real object all the while is religion and morality,
though you appear to be attending to other things. This is the true
and only way to succeed.'" However slow Protestant teachers are
in learning this principle, Roman Catholics are by no means deficient

immortality consists. In pursuing this end, means strictly analogous to the Divine dealings with man in the scheme of redemption are to be employed. The instructor must regard himself as standing in God's stead to the child; the Divine dealings with man, particularly as illustrated in the life of the Redeemer, present the model by which his dealings with the pupil are to be regulated. As by the revelation of God's love the spiritual transformation of man *is* accomplished, so must the earthly teacher build all his moral agencies on the manifestation of his own love towards the pupil. Then, as "we love God because He first loved us," so will the affections of the pupil be awakened towards his instructor, when he feels himself the object of that instructor's regard.* Again, as love to God generates

in applying it. An attempt to carry it out is made by ourselves in this Institution in Lessons on Scripture Natural History.

* The means of making education essentially religious are the teacher's spirit and character, her general management and discipline, a sense of the Divine presence in the minds of the children, and instruction. The power of religion should be seen in every department of the teacher's school-life. It should regulate her *temper*, guide her in her *work*, strengthen her in her *difficulties*. She should come to her school *imbued with the sentiments of true religion*, which will lead her to love her young charges, to take pleasure in mingling with them, and to act simply and condescendingly towards them. Her *self-denial*, which will lead her to be watchful against her failings, and to avoid caprice and partiality,

conformity to His will, so will obedience to the instructor be the consequence of awakened affection. This is the basis of a right education ; for as " *love* is the fulfilment of the law," so in *love* must be sought the elements which, in this fulfilment, have their ultimate result. Thus, while other modes of instruction may convey the *doctrines* of Christianity, the system of Pestalozzi, equally adapted

should lead the children to respect religion by respecting her. Her gentleness and sweetness should lead them to love it and her in return. *Her bright cheerful countenance*, the result of peace within and a spirit of good-will to all, should teach them that religion ensures happiness. In this way would she win souls to Christ. On other means of making religion essential in school-work, Dr. Mayo remarks, that "the God of nature is to be seen in His works, the God of all grace contemplated in His written Word, and felt in His influence. A sense of the continual presence of God as the Giver of all good, and the Judge of all conduct, must be made a pervading sentiment in the minds of the pupils." To carry this out, at all lessons in physical science, as in geography, natural history, natural objects and phenomena, not only must the power and wisdom of God be exhibited, but the truth that He is good to all, and His tender mercies are over all His works. Such lessons without reference to God are very defective. At the Bible lessons, the character of God in its bearing on the wants, character, and condition of man, as a sinner, must be amply displayed. A sense of God's goodness will lead to love and gratitude, of His greatness and power to reverence and admiration, and of His presence as a judge to holy reverence and watchful conduct. Thus by the operation of the Blessed Spirit, God will be felt in His sacred influence.

to the attainment of this result, is also, when duly executed, a practical illustration of its *temper* and *spirit.**

Principle 2. — *Education should be essentially moral.*† The principles and standard of its morality

* Education will never fulfil its Heaven-appointed mission until the essential and pervading character of religion is recognized as one of its best instruments. This is certainly the "training" which is enjoined on parents, and on teachers who are their coadjutors, or substitutes. Where it is adopted, the power of influence, of example, of association will come to our help, and be confirmed into habit, which will, by God's grace, be matured into principle.

† What is *moral* education? wherein does it differ from *religious* education? Dr. Mayo distinguishes them from, yet connects them with, each other; not a few would completely separate them. It may therefore be useful to young teachers to give them an accurate idea of "moral" as applied in education, and then to ask them whether they could conscientiously teach morality without the Bible, without religion. The term moral is variously applied in connection with the work of the teacher.

(1.) It means good, virtuous, honest, &c., as opposed to the terms immoral, vicious, or bad. In this sense moral instruction includes reasoning, expostulating, pointing out both what is virtuous and what is vicious, and to the practice of the one and abstention from indulgence in the other. All are agreed on this point.

(2.) The term moral is used as relating to the conduct of men to each other, in contradistinction to the term religious, which relates to the duties of men towards God. It is in this sense that the term describes a subject of instruction in our schools.

should be derived from the precepts of the Gospel, as
illustrated by the example of the Redeemer, and in-

In this sense, too, we may have morality without religion,
whilst we cannot have true religion without morality. In many
schools the instruction is religious, whilst the training is merely
moral. Alas! there is a growing party in this country which
desires to divorce religion from morality in the school, both
in theory and practice. And we have been asked to accept "Ethics
for Board Schools" as a guide to teachers out of "the Religious
Difficulty"—a treatise which inculcates morality without any
recognition of religion as its basis.

(3.) The term moral is applied to the doctrine or duty drawn
from a story, a fable, or a parable ; and no good teacher will fail to
turn fiction to this profitable use.

(4.) Another meaning of the term is that of "subject to the
moral law." Hence we are said to possess moral responsibility ; a
condition which every pious teacher will explain to his
pupils as they increase in intelligence, and thus endeavour,
by God's blessing, to make them realize the mainspring of
duty.

(5.) Again, moral is used in opposition to animal or physical,
as in the expression "moral courage," that is the courage of
moral principle, not that of the animal passions or brute force.
This distinction an intelligent teacher will not fail to make in
training children, giving to each its place in the scale of moral
excellence.

(6.) The term moral as used in the science of education
relates to the feelings, as distinguished from the intellect, which
has reference to the thoughts. This application of the term is in
accordance with the primary signification of the word, which means
manners or conduct, and is an appropriate application, since conduct
in general, particularly in the case of children, proceeds from the

culcated throughout the Bible.* Moral instruction, to be availing, must be the purified and elevated

feelings rather than from reflection. It is on the same ground that the plural noun "morals" is used for the practice of the duties of life.

(7.) "Moral" has also the meaning of "probable" as applied to evidence, as opposed to "absolute" or "certain." Hence it is that we speak of "moral" or "absolute" certainty ; and the teacher has his two great classes of subjects of instruction, the moral and the absolute, as history and mathematics, &c., with which to cultivate and store the minds of his pupils.

* The morality which, according to Dr. Mayo, should form an essential element of education, was fully and clearly expressed by Mr. Ogle in an address to our students and teachers at one of their half-yearly meetings. "By *morality*," he said, "we do not in this Institution mean merely that ordinary good conduct which men may practise from natural constitution, or from the force of a good education, or from good example. Neither do we mean, when we speak of giving moral lessons, the giving the children at one hour a Scripture lesson, in which we teach them the principles and precepts of the religion of Christ, and at another hour a moral lesson, for example, on perseverance, or on filial love, or on humanity—speaking of these as if there were no such Being as our Lord and Saviour Jesus Christ and His Gospel, precisely as a heathen philosopher might do. We have no such view before us. By morality we mean that practice which results from obedience to Christian precepts, which is founded on Christian principles, the application to the ordinary events and duties of life, of the doctrines and precepts of the Christian religion. And in our moral instruction and training we apply to children in their ordinary conduct, in the schoolroom and playground, the precepts which they learn from the Bible. Thus education, to be essentially moral, should be derived from the precepts of the Gospel, as illustrated by the example of the Lord Jesus, and conducted on the principles of the Word of God."

expression of a moral life, actually pervading the
scene of education.*   In carrying on the business of

* It is not enough that the moral lessons be regularly given,
systematically, even impressively delivered. They must be illustrations of the teacher's own life, in order to reach readily both the
understanding and heart. It is a happy thing when the teacher
can refer to himself as walking by the rule which he lays down,
since the sight of such consistency will inspire the children with
willing readiness to imitate. It is happier still when the children
feel that their teacher is a model of all the social virtues. Such a
feeling calls out their sympathy, excites reverence and love, and
leads to unfailing obedience. The example and spirit of the pupils
have also great influence. If rudeness, violence, untruth, and
injustice prevail amongst them, the moral instruction will be un-
availing ; every good desire excited will be stifled by the impure
atmosphere around them.   But the teacher has the tone of the
school very much at his own command. It is a point to which a
good teacher will give every attention, and he will not rest till the
public opinion of the school is on the side of gentleness, goodness,
and truth.

Moreover, moral education includes the *active training* of the
pupils and the direct cultivation of the moral nature. Nothing is
more common than to mistake moral and religious instruction for
religious and moral training, and to be satisfied with the former.
The only moral culture worthy of the name is that which consists in
leading children to act. Instruction is of course necessary, as a
child must be taught what is right in order to practise it ; but is not
sufficient, any more than is the theory of music to make a man a
musician, or a knowledge of perspective or of lights and shades to
make a man a painter. Between the knowledge of what is right
and the doing what is right there are two stages, feeling and volition.
We must know, feel, and will. Action is the only real education in
morals. Moral conduct and moral habits are to be secured by

the schoolroom, or in watching over the diversions of the playground, the motives and restraints of the purest morality, and those only, must be employed.* Moral diseases are not to be counteracted by moral poisons; nor is intellectual attainment to be furthered at the expense of moral good."† Under the

training up a child in the way he should go, not merely by teaching him. A great mistake is often made by religious parents on this point, and they compare unfavourably in this respect with many people of the world. They do not consider that whilst moral principles cannot exist without religion, moral habits may. Now parents who are religious generally confine their attention to the former. From an exclusive zeal to establish moral principle, they are often guilty of neglecting moral habits—their children *hear* rather than *do*. Thus we may account for the unhappy abnormal state of the children of many of the disciples of Christianity; a state of things bearing a striking contrast to the disciples of Judaism. The children of light are in this respect not wise in their generation.

* In dealing with children, whether in repressing or punishing for evil done, or in encouraging, stimulating, and rewarding for good done, teachers are continually rousing motives for action or acting on those in operation. These motives are of very different kinds; some are high, some low, some selfish and bad, others generous and pure. Therefore in carrying on the business of the schoolroom, or watching the diversions of the playground, the teacher should only employ those motives and restraints which are of the purest and highest morality.

† Place-taking stirs up an ignoble ambition. Prizes and rewards bring into operation covetousness, which is already too strong. Partiality and putting children in opposition to each other also stir up envy, jealousy, and hatred. It is at the expense of moral good

conditions of the organic character of education will be found additional remarks on this last point.

*Principle 3. — " Education should be essentially organic.** A stone increases in size by the mechanical deposition of matter on its external surface; a plant, on the other hand, grows by

that a teacher bestows more attention upon learning than conduct, is more pleased with cleverness than goodness, presents more and greater stimuli to the learning of lessons than the practice of virtues, and rewards the exercise of the intellect and not the dispositions of the heart. Throughout all this there is evidence of the intellectual teacher rather than of the moral educator.

* The organic character of true education springs from the organic nature of the mind, which is the subject of education. The human soul is not a uniform and inert mass of being, but a living, active structure, an organism of the highest order. The means used to educate it must obviously be suited to its nature ; the mind must be dealt with as an organized existence. It has laws by which it exists, develops, and improves, and its treatment in harmony with these laws constitutes an organic education. The term is therefore used by Dr. Mayo metonymically ; the instrument being put for the object on which it operates. The organic character of education was the fundamental principle of the system of Pestalozzi, and from it sprang most of his other principles, such as : 1. That education must be progressive, commencing with a natural and well-laid foundation. 2. That education must be spontaneous, the child being a willing co-operator with the teacher. 3. That each faculty must be developed carefully, gradually, steadily. 4. That education must be an entire work, embracing the hand, the head, and the heart. 5. That education must be harmonious.

the continual expansion of those organs which lie folded up in its germ. Elementary education, as ordinarily carried on, is a *mechanical* inculcation of knowledge, the process being similar to that by which a mineral substance is increased, that of accretion. In the Pestalozzian system it is an *organic* development of the human faculties—moral, intellectual, and physical—from within by a process of expansion or growth. Moral education does not consist in preventing immoral actions in the pupil, but in cultivating dispositions, forming principles, and establishing habits. Nor does intellectual education attain its end by the mere communication of intellectual truths, but rather in the development of those faculties by which truth is recognized and distinguished. And, lastly, physical education, instead of confining itself to instruction in particular arts, must be directed to the improvement of the outward senses, the increase of activity and strength, and those circumstances which are essential to the promotion of health.

"Organic education has its conditions—these are activity and liberty. *Activity* is the great means of development, for action is the parent of power. The sentiments of the heart, the faculties of the mind, the powers of the body, advance to their maturity through a succession of actings in conformity to their nature; *i.e.*, all are strengthened by exercise and dwindle through inactivity. Opportunities for the exercise of moral virtue should therefore be carefully sought out, or at least diligently applied. To cultivate benevolent dispositions, the pupil should be invited to relieve the indigent; to overcome his selfishness, he should be induced to share or part with the objects of his own desire. In intellectual culture every branch of instruction should be so presented to the pupil's mind as to bring into the highest activity the faculties most legitimately employed upon it.

" That there may be that action that leads to development there must be *liberty*. The pupil should have sufficient liberty to manifest decidedly his individual character, and must be dealt with accordingly. Nothing short of this will render the education really organic.* It may be possible, by a system of coercion, to produce a negative exterior morality which shall endure as long as the

---

* But this liberty is perfectly consistent with natural and proper restraint. It is so with the body. The body contains physical ligaments and bands, but they do not obstruct action. Artificial ligaments tighten the feet, the fingers, or the body. So it is morally and intellectually, where necessary restraint is not united with the liberty of action that promotes growth.

circumstances on which it is built remain in force; but no interior moral power, that shall survive a change of outward circumstances, can be formed, unless such moral liberty be enjoyed as leaves to the judgment room for discerning between good and evil; to the moral choice the adoption of the one and the rejection of the other; to the conscience the approval and the rewarding of right, the condemnation and punishment of wrong. Restraint may be necessary to prevent wrong, to check the career of passion, to arrest the progress and diffusion of moral mischief, to remove the incentives to evil, and to restore to that position in which the moral principle may again exert its influence. Still it is only a negative, not a positive means. All the real development of man, moral, intellectual, and physical, arises from moral, intellectual, and physical *liberty*. Human laws, guarded by vindictive enactments, may be respected even by slaves; but the law of God, wheresoever and in so far as it is obeyed, is written in the hearts of a willing people in the enjoyments of Christian liberty."*—*Dr. Mayo.

---

* It is a great mistake to confound negation and restraint with positive training; yet how frequently are prohibitions and punishments regarded as all that are necessary in the moral education of the young. In restraining children from wrong-doing we are far from teaching them to do what

Principle 4.—-*"Education must be directed by an influence essentially parental.* Where there is no mother there can be no child, is as true morally as it is physically. It is the order of providence that maternal affection and maternal wisdom should call forth the dawning powers of childhood, and that the wisdom and firmness of a father should build up and consolidate the fabric which reposes on a mother's love. The Pestalozzian instructor supplying the parent's place must combine the characters of each relation, but exhibit them in different proportions, according to the age and disposition of his pupil. Other plans of education are built on the principles of political relations, the system of Pestalozzi carries in its bosom the pure and gentle influence of domestic life. There the glowing affections, the fearless confidence, the easy intercourse, the gentle spirit, of the family circle are

is right. They are merely debarred from choice, and have, no part or lot in the matter of right and wrong except as passive instruments. All moral actions spring from motives ; these act through the will, and choice becomes necessary for us as moral and responsible beings. But if our children are so restrained that they cannot choose whether they will act on a right or wrong motive, or so constrained that they are not in the habit of choosing, how can their moral nature be undergoing the process of training? Punishments are restraints, *i.e.*, not direct and positive means of producing moral good, but merely negative forces. The real use of punishment is to deter a child from doing evil, not to induce him to do good.

transplanted into a field of greater extent, but of congenial soil; and the delicate bloom of moral sensibility, which the rude contact of the playground seldom fails to destroy, is watched over with care, and sheltered with tenderness."*—*Dr. Mayo.*

* The family character of the school was a principle that Pestalozzi held with great tenacity, and placed next to that of the organic character of education. We are better acquainted in this country with the intellectual side of Pestalozzianism, than with the moral; with its methods of teaching, than with the spirit of government which animated it. But the schoolmaster who can only teach intelligently, develop ideas, and discipline the intellectual powers is but half a Pestalozzian. Without the parental spirit there is no true Pestalozzianism; there may be instruction, but not education. To lead to the clearer apprehension of this principle, it may be remarked that there are four different kinds of rule, differing from each other in spirit and character. There is, first, military rule, which is characterized by severity. There is, secondly, political rule, characterized by what is formal, almost mechanical, and often aided by planning and plotting. Justice is done, but in the way of business or policy, and whilst giving a sense of security and exciting no malignant passion, such government cherishes little that is attaching, elevating, or improving. There is, thirdly, parental rule, which alone comes from the heart and goes to the heart. It is marked by the *interest* that is ever watchful of good to the child; of the *tenderness* that sympathizes with and even anticipates the child's sorrows and joys; of the *patience* that does not readily murmur, is never weary in well-doing for the child, and often hoping against hope. Then, fourthly, there is pastoral rule, which unites watchfulness, diligence, faithfulness, and kindness. It springs from benevolence, a sense of duty, and Christian devotedness, but it has none of the instinctive love of the mother. As Dr.

Principle 5.—" The development of the faculties should be harmonious. In some cases the intellectual

Mayo tells us in the text, other plans of education are based on the principle of political relations, whilst the system of Pestalozzi carries in its bosom the gentle loveliness of domestic life. Would that we had more of this spirit in our schools, then would the teacher merit the endearing title of Father, by which Pestalozzi frequently was known among his pupils.

The origin or history of this principle is interesting and instructive. The longer Pestalozzi persevered in his efforts at Neuhof, the firmer grew his conviction that education was the only hopeful means of permanently improving the people, and emancipating them from the thraldom of ignorance, vice, and oppression. But the more he gave himself up to these ideas, the more did he feel the necessity of something more influential than any system of instruction, however interesting, or of discipline, however rigid and productive of order. In fact, he had no faith in mere external sources for elevating the degraded and permanently blessing all. Pestalozzi not only had faith in an education which would reach and influence the principles of human nature, but he felt persuaded that it was an appointed means of God for the happiness and holiness of His creatures.

Having arrived at these conclusions, it next occurred to him that in the wise arrangements of God there must somewhere be found the natural sphere of education, provided with the necessary power for accomplishing the ends in view. He consequently cast about for some ground the most extensive and some power the most irresistible by which to animate the new system of improvement. Then the thought occurred that the earliest, most extensive, best *adapted sphere* for education is the domestic circle, in which the infant and early years are spent; but, alas! often without the benefit of a kind and salutary direction, and frequently under the baneful influence of bad example. It also occurred to him that the most or moral, or both, are sacrificed to the physical ; in some the moral, or physical, or both, to the intel-

energetic power in the whole range of the moral world was sympathy and affection ; and that of all human sympathies and affections, the purest and strongest was maternal love.   This was the power to be gained for the great object which he had in view.   The family was the fulcrum, the mother's love the lever by which the philosopher of Zurich would obtain power to move the moral world. In a nobler cause than that of the ancient mathematican might he exclaim, *Eurēka, Eurēka!* Henceforth his maxim was, "Where there is no mother, there is no child, morally as well as physically." The training of mothers to do their duty intelligently and effectually was the subject of his strongest advocacy.   In his letters to Greaves he gives expression to his feelings in eloquent strains.   Let mothers and teachers hear him on this topic.   "I do not anticipate," he says, "half the advantages to mankind, as long as our system of improvement fails of reaching the earliest stage of education ; and to succeed in this we require the most powerful ally of our cause.   This object of our ardent desires will only be attained through the assistance of mothers.   To them we must appeal ; with them we must pray for the blessing of Heaven ; in them try to awaken a deep sense of all the consequences, of all the self-denial, and of all the rewards attached to their interesting duties."   The estimate which Pestalozzi formed of this prize, and the place which he assigned it in his system, ought to be thoroughly realized.   It inspired him with the most sanguine hopes ; it was from that moment the centre of all his efforts, the foundation of his system of moral influence and moral elevation.   But in time Pestalozzi became dissatisfied here, and he then made his grand final discovery.   He would carry the parental feeling into the schoolroom, and convert the schoolroom into a home.   He saw that the family was the original school — God's model school from the beginning.   The trainers of children, according to the order of nature, are their

lectual. A Pestalozzian educator respects the
rights of each. He fortifies the body by gym-

parents, their brothers and sisters. Henceforth his motto was,
"School are families on a large scale." His thoughts might be expressed in the following formula :—That as the family is the
nursing-place of society, Heaven's own ordained means of rearing
up to all that is great and good, and the mother's love is given to
secure that end, education must be of a family character and conducted under the influence of the maternal spirit—a thinking love.

The parental spirit of the schoolmistress should be no matter of
accident. It ought not to depend merely upon impulse, nor be
mere matter of imitation, but ought to be felt as a necessity from
the nature of the case, and as a matter of principle based on the
most cogent arguments. 1st. It is reasonable. The schoolmistress
has taken the parent's place to a great extent, and consequently has
involved herself in the parent's responsibilities. Pestalozzi
demanded that those who undertook the parent's duties should
possess the parent's spirit in its *interest* in the best welfare of the
child ; in its sympathy with its joys and sorrows ; in the *patience*
which will not flag or murmur. Nor did Pestalozzi merely preach
this as a doctrine, but practised it himself. 2nd. Nature calls for it.
We cannot expect the confidence of a child, unless we show somewhat of the loving feelings of the mother ; nor the affectionate
obedience of the child, unless we show somewhat of the tender
watchfulness of the mother ; nor the gratitude of the child, where
there is not the persevering care of the mother. God has ordained
the one for the other. We are very exacting at the hands of
children, forgetting that we ourselves have a part to act. Our
treatment of the child and the character springing up in him
correspond as cause and effect. Deficiencies in the training of the
child must ever produce corresponding deficiencies in his character.
Witness the absence of emotions in children reared in orphanages,
where, with all the kindness experienced they lack maternal interest,

nastic exercises, while he cultivates the understanding and trains the sentiments.* He endeavours

maternal tenderness, and maternal patience. 3rd. This spirit will give a particular tone to the rewards and punishments of the school. Punishments will be administered with sorrow rather than anger ; and the future good of the children considered rather than the present convenience of the teacher. Attention to their wants will be given with kindly interest ; mischievous rivalry in the shape of place-taking and similar practices will never be adopted·; mutual help will be encouraged instead of a spirit of triumph at each other's failures. The parental spirit will inspire with gentleness towards the timid, patience with the slow, and compassion for those labouring under physical or other defects. 4th. In God and in Christ we have this spirit pre-eminently exhibited. Amongst the various names taken by God is that of Father. The love of the former is illustrated in the father of the prodigal, the love of Christ was displayed in apologizing for His poor remiss disciples, praying for His enemies, and pleading their ignorance as their excuse. 5th. 'The parental idea is the grand feature of Pestalozzianism ; it was a leading idea of Pestalozzi himself; and he not only felt, but practised it. Let every teacher strive to realize the weight and tenderness of a relation which combines the parent with the pastor. Let parental interest, tenderness, and patience be united with pastoral watchfulness, diligence, and faithfulness.

* The principle would be more exactly stated thus :—" *Education should be an entire work.*" It should be a complete system, regulating and training the entire being, meeting all his wants, circumstances, and character. Education to be thus complete must be fivefold, so as to meet the fivefold nature of the child. 1. It must be *Physical*, to meet the requirements of his bodily nature ; 2. *Intellectual*, for the cultivation and storing of the powers of thought ; 3. *Esthetical* in relation to the sense of the beautiful ; 4. *Moral*, for the feelings, and the conduct in relation to man ; and 5. *Spiritual*, to

to preserve the equipoise in each, as well as between all the three departments ; to mingle firmness with sweetness, judgment with taste, activity with strength. His object will be, not to develop a disproportionate strength in one faculty, but to produce that general harmony of mind and character which is the most conducive to the happiness and usefulness of the individual." *—*Dr. Mayo.*

meet the wants of the soul in reference to God. Pestalozzi would have considered any system of education defective which neglected the faculties under any of these divisions. It would not be an entire work, and the pupil would be but partially benefited.

The connection between this secondary principle and the great fundamental principle of the organic nature of education may be stated as follows :—As education is of an organic character, and all the faculties and powers of the child are essential to his well-being, it should be complete and entire, and its business should be to develop and perfect all the elements of the child's nature.

* This is not mere universality of cultivation, but harmony, which consists of a fitting together of parts, so as to form a connected whole—not a mere equipoise, but a concord. Education would be an entire work, were the faculties cultivated by it singly, as if independent of each other ; but it is harmonious when they are cultivated, not in opposition to each other, but in their organic connection, all working together to produce one result. The importance of the application of this principle in education may be easily demonstrated. There is no doubt that harmony originally subsisted among the elements of man's nature. By the Fall, however, man became depraved, that is, changed from a good state to a bad. Speaking metaphysically, not theologically, this change consisted, not only in the faculties becoming excessive, deficient, or mis-

That true education consists in the harmonious
development of all the faculties with which man is

directed, but also in their proportion and harmony being destroyed.
In the Restoration of man this proportion and harmony must be ·
restored. The necessity of harmonious operation is beautifully exhibited in the figure of the Apostle, in which he compares the
members of the Christian Church to the members of the human
body, and urges that each has a specific work to perform, whilst all
derive their power from the same source, and all should contribute
to one end by mutual co-operation. Again, in architecture, proportion is beauty, and parts mutually aid and support each other, in
order to form a harmonious whole. In physiology, too, it is only as
the organs of the body are brought into activity in their natural
connection and dependence, that the strength, completeness, and
health of the body are secured. The design of education is, in like
manner, to establish unity and harmony in man ; unity of purpose
promoted by harmony of operation in reference to both time and
eternity, to God and man, leading us to ascribe glory to the one,
and perform offices of good-will to the other. Thus would be
produced that balanced character which is the result of harmonious
development. This harmonious development has reference to three
things—1st. *To the elements of the child's nature.* With regard
to his moral nature, the lower feelings must be brought into
subjection to the moral sentiments, as they were evidently designed
to be. The moral sentiments must be under the dominion of the
conscience, which is the candle of the Lord, searching all the
inward parts. The feelings, desires, affections, even the conscience
must be enlightened by the intellect from the altar of sacred
truth, and both reason and conscience, thus enlightened, must
be brought under the dominion of God, *i.e.*, under subjection
to His will. In reference to *the intellect,*. its perfection seems
mainly to consist in the proper adjustment of the observing, the
reflecting, and imaginative faculties—in other words, of the powers

gifted, is continually asserted by Pestalozzi, who endeavours to prove it in the following way. He

by which the knowledge of things exterior to ourselves is acquired; and the powers by which that knowledge is turned to account, either in the new combinations of fancy or deductions of reason. An unusual deficiency in either stamps the whole intellectual character with defect and antagonism, if not with imbecility. *2nd. To the end of the child's being in lifetime*, whether he is to be agriculturist, artizan, merchant, professional man, or prince. Such a training of the faculties should be given as will enable him to move in his future position with pleasure and advantage to himself and his fellow-men. Diversity of sex, and consequent difference of future occupations, come under this head, demanding modification in the education of different individuals. *3rd. To the last and highest end of man*, which is perfect harmony and eternal union with God. To assist in effecting this, cultivation must be so conducted and blessed by the Spirit of God, that all the child's powers, whether of body or soul, may be rendered subservient to this great purpose, and co-operate to effect it. In the training of immortal beings for eternity, no minor end must be allowed to engross attention. At the same time it must not be forgotten that the battle for eternity is to be fought in the field of the world, and, consequently, the young are to be prepared for the world. Secular instruction is not inconsistent with religious teaching; and those who would reduce the amount of secular instruction to the smallest possible amount, teaching religion almost exclusively, make a great mistake. Religion includes within its sphere the religious performance of duty, not only in relation to God, but also to man. And to perform our duties to man, we must be qualified to discharge them as intelligent and responsible beings, possessing a personal concern and interest in what they do, whether for others or for themselves.

The methods by which the teacher may promote this equilibrium

declares that it is the proper business of education
to develop the man, to keep in view all his faculties,

are various—1. An *entire education*, if judiciously conducted, will
contribute to give the energetic hand, the clear head, and the
warm heart, which, united in the cause of well-doing, exhibit
glorious harmony. 2. In educating children, never lose sight of
certain leading powers, for on their cultivation the harmony to be
secured will, humanly speaking, depend. These are conscience,
the natural arbiter of the will and ruler of the internal
life ; reason or judgment, the conscience of things intellectual ;
taste, the conscience of things beautiful ; and faith working by love.
These being in all children especially cultivated, other qualities may,
as it were, be suffered to blend into them and in the prominence and
proportion assigned to them by the character of the individual
mind to which they belong. Conscience, reason, taste, and love
may be likened to the essential notes of a musical composition,
which are always there, and sometimes in fixed positions; yet far
from causing monotony, they blend harmoniously into the less
essential notes, softening and enriching the most varied and ex-
quisite strains, and adding to the character and originality of each
individual melody. 3. Care must be taken not to put down with
one hand what is built with the other. Mistakes are daily made
in this respect by both parents and teachers. For instance, attempts
are often made to remove sinful passions. But how ? Often by the
encouragement of others that are worse. We encourage selfishness
in children by our system of prizes and place-taking, &c. ; and then
with an inconsistency hardly accountable, we are disappointed at our
own success. Admitting the superiority of the moral nature to the
intellectual, and that it is the former that has suffered most by the
Fall, we, notwithstanding, sacrifice moral to intellectual improvement ;
we send our children to school to *think* rather than to *feel*, to
know rather than to *act*, and to acquire a smattering of crude ideas
rather than the habits and principles that best fit for a life of

N

to aim at their culture and perfection, not singly and apart from each other, but as a whole, and by a simultaneous though gradual process. A child is endowed with all the faculties of human nature, but undeveloped—*a bud not yet opened.* When the bud expands every leaf unfolds, not one remains behind. Similar to this should be the process of education ; no faculty of human nature but must be treated with attention, for their co-agency is necessary to ensure success.*

happiness, usefulness, and piety. We find children remarkable for the activity and strength of some faculty, whilst deficient in those of others. We designate such disproportionate beings geniuses, and have them educated as if all the other faculties were to be absorbed into those already too strong. Only particular studies are engaged in, only congenial exercises attended to. The child is to become a great poet, painter, musician, or engineer, and consequently everything not directly contributing to that end is rejected. The distortions of nature are thus increased, a caricature upon humanity is produced, or the individual comes out into life a piece of conceit or eccentricity, fitter to boast than to execute, the object of occasional envy or constant contempt. To escape such results let us attend to the harmonious development of the faculties, and experience its beneficial consequences.

* Many English educators have propounded this principle of education, but it remained for Pestalozzi to give it due form, and impart to it a practical bearing. Dugald Stewart, the distinguished author of the " Philosophy of the Human Mind," thus describes it :—

"The essential objects of education are, first, to cultivate the various principles of our nature, both speculative and active, in such a

Pestalozzi was accustomed to look at man under a
threefold aspect, as a moral, an intellectual, and a

manner as to bring them to the greatest perfection of which they
are capable ; secondly, by watching over the impressions which the
mind receives in early life to secure it against the influence of prevailing errors, and to engage its prepossessions on the side of
truth." According to Dr. Whewell, education is not merely the
acquisition of a certain amount of knowledge, but such a training
of the human powers as may render them capable of vigorous
exercise. All education is imperfect, "in which the attainment of
these ends is not made the prominent object. If the reason be exclusively cultivated to the disregard of the other faculties, the
education is imperfect ; if the faculty of language is the exclusive
subject of culture, the education is illiberal, though hundreds a year
may have been expended to procure it. A liberal education is not
a partial, but a universal development of the faculties of man."
Another writer says :—" I call that education which embraces the
culture of the whole man—subjecting his senses, his understanding,
and his passions to reason, to conscience, and to the laws of the
Christian revelation. In character, as in architecture, proportion is
beauty, therefore let there be proportionate culture of all the parts
of the human being." And Mme. Necker de Saussure, in her
" Progressive Education," says :—It has almost always happened
that instructors have been too much influenced by partial views.
They have not troubled themselves about the cultivation of the
faculties when communicating their instructions ; and when convinced by experience of the necessity, they have still overlooked the
importance of preserving these different faculties in harmony with
each other. Sometimes the memory has been cultivated, while the
imagination has been entirely neglected ; sometimes the faculty of
investigation has been invested with such high powers that it has
been thought possible for the pupil to discover for himself all the
wonders of science, so making no use of the stores of knowledge

corporeal being. Hence his practical axiom—Education is to deal with the heart, the head, and the hand. How shall their expanding faculties be directed? Which of them call for the most diligent attention? Which have the most important bearings on the future welfare of the child?

Pestalozzi rightly considered that the last question must be decided in favour of those of the heart, that it had the first and especially prominent claim to attention. He compared it to the spring of a watch, or the main wheel in a piece of complicated machinery; and yet a teacher or parent may be puzzled as to the relative importance of different faculties, and the consequent proportion of attention they separately demand. "But what can be the use of the utmost possible exertions, unless regulated by accuracy of ideas, correct judgment, and, above all, the control of a firm and steady will? What, again, can be the real use and merit of schemes, however deep or ingenious, if the energy or exertion be not equal to the boldness and skill of conception; or even if these are combined, but are not working for an end worthy of themselves, and beneficial to humanity?

accumulated by time. And thus it will be, as long as the attention of the instructor is bestowed more upon the science he wishes to teach than on the pupil who is to be taught; as long as he is more desirous to form a living encyclopædia than an intellectual and moral being."

" It is obvious, then, that a mere cultivation of the faculties of our animal and intellectual nature will be found absolutely insufficient as a substitute for those of the heart. But again, we may suppose the case of one full of good intentions, his heart overflowing with amiable dispositions, and his zeal ever ready to patronize and promote any enterprise that has for its object the good of society. This constellation of excellences may glow and sparkle in vain; such a temperament, however finely constituted, may yet live to little purpose in reference to others. The reason is obvious; the heart, the grand wheel in the human mechanism, may have been long and actively at work, but for want of being connected in due time with those other powers of human nature whose co-operation is equally essential, it has failed of producing that health and vitality which would otherwise have pervaded the system. The faculties of man must, in fact, be so cultivated that one shall not predominate at the expense of another, but each be excited to its true standard of activity."

The recognition of this fundamental principle, which Pestalozzi so clearly propounded, led to quite new views on the subject, and he sought to introduce and establish a more effective and enlightened system of popular education.

How shall the expanding faculties be exercised and

directed ? The great means to be employed in moral development Pestalozzi held to be love. The mother's love draws out the child's love ; the mother's care and tenderness awaken the first dawnings of faith ; the child feels safe in her arms ; he confides in her word ; what she says he believes ; and her will is the law to which he yields and which he obeys. Thus it is in the mother's arms that the moral character is first developed, and moral education passes its first stage. Rightly to direct and exercise the nascent faculties and sentiments, is the next point; and here, God himself, our heavenly Father, as early as possible, must be presented as the first object of love—His superintending providence as the object of faith, and His will as the rule of life. Thus, as we have seen, moral faculties are first called forth by the circum- stances with which God has surrounded the child. But the impulse thus given to these faculties must be directed and controlled by precepts deduced from revelation, and the conscience trained to recognize and acknowledge these precepts ; so that constant shortcomings being thus made evident, the child may be prepared to listen to a Saviour's love as manifested in His wondrous work of man's redemption.*

* Not only love, but the whole of the moral faculties of the child must be brought into exercise in order to make education an entire work. *The social feelings* should be drawn out by the presence of

It is hardly possible to conceive the blighting chill
which the affections receive when the child is trans-

companions, *the love of approbation* by praise, *the love of activity* by
giving plenty of work to do, *the love of home* by making it happy,
and by giving school a family character ; *caution* should be cultivated by warning against danger, *benevolence* by presenting objects
of pity, *courage* by accustoming to brave opposition and evil, *respect*
by presenting venerable objects, *conscience* by presenting right and
wrong, &c., &c. *The intellect* should be cultivated by the discipline
of varied thought kept in vigorous exercise. The observation must
be exercised in every direction until it becomes acute. Habitual
attention must be brought into operation until it becomes concen-
trated and sustained. The power of *simple suggestion* must be
systematically used, not merely in the acquisition of knowledge, but
for the purpose of creating those early associations which have a
lasting effect on the tastes and character. The faculties of conception and imagination should be exercised until the former attains to
clearness and versatility, and the latter to the power of apprehending
the imagery of the poet and the painter, and of making creations of
its own. *Memory* must be in regular operation, laying up its stores
and recalling them at will, until it becomes retentive, ready, and
faithful. The powers of *abstraction* and *generalization* which convert the child into the man must, in due time and degree, be exercised, that separate facts may be changed into general truth, the
essentials of things be comprehended through their accidentals, and
principles through details. Next to imagination these faculties form
new creations, and raise above the varying hues of the real into
those of the idealistic and the unchangeable. The faculties of judgment and the reasoning powers must be called out on their appropriate objects, both of contingent and absolute truth, the former in
the regions of physical, mechanical, and social science, morals, and
history ; and the latter on form and number in their various qualiti
and applications to both science and art. Finally, as to the physical

erred from the warm sunshine of a mother's love to a teacher who governs by fear, works by machinery, and rules with the rod.   This is the source of many a moral failure.   The true Pestalozzian is not a teacher of this class.   On the contrary, he presents himself at all times to his pupils in the parental character; and by practically evincing to them that their welfare and comfort are wisely and steadily pursued, confidence is inspired ; and confidence habitually felt gives an amiable, noble frankness, and an unsuspicious fearlessness of character.   He regards coercion and 'restraint as evils, but, having to deal with a fallen and perverse nature in his pupils, he sees that they are necessary evils ; he therefore allows as much liberty as is compatible with a healthy discipline.*   On this point Dr. Mayo's eloquent remarks

nature of the child, the corporeal powers must be developed and strengthened by a system of gymnastic and other exercises, so arranged as to bring all the organs of the body into play.   To carry this out there must be a playground, with variety of apparatus to afford exercise to all the muscles of the body.   The teacher must superintend and encourage the exercises with as much regularity as she attends to other departments of her duty.   Moreover, she must complete the work of physical education by attending to the conditions of health and activity, such as good air, light, temperature, ventilation, cleanliness, change of posture, marching, singing, &c. Wholesome food and proper clothing, however necessary to physical well-being, are not under the control of teachers.

*A successful education cannot be brought about by mere human have already been introduced in connection with "organic education."

*Principle 6.—Education should be of a mixed character.**

wisdom and skill, nor by the contemplation of the God of nature, and obedience to His voice in creation and providence. This will never suffice to bring peace with God, with self, or with mankind, so long as the fatal disease of sin rules in man's nature; as the placing of the best-tuned organ before a performer whose hands are paralyzed, or whose ear is untrue, will prove insufficient to bring forth harmonious sounds. A power is required mighty enough to enlighten man's eyes, and to purify his heart, so as to enable him to look at creation in the true light, and to understand the invisible things of God by the things that are visible. This power can only be found in the Gospel of the crucified and risen Son of God. It is well that our children should, as it were, bathe in the rivers of creation, but they must also bathe in the ocean of Divine truth— the Scriptures, by which the Gospel of the grace of God is communicated. Thus, to the voice of nature will be added the voice of revelation. But the direction given to moral training will depend as much on the system of education as on the religious principles of the educator.

* In her summary of the principles of Pestalozzi, Miss Mayo gives this a distinct place. It might be thus fully stated—That, as the faculties of children are various, and the ends to be accomplished equally so; as perfection of character can only be secured and the business of life accomplished by the vigour and activity of the various faculties of the human being, education should be of a mixed character. Miss Mayo maintained that education should be practical as well as preceptive, illustrated by the teacher as well as enforced upon the child, and applied both individually and collectively; that it should also be practical, by drawing much of

Principle 7. — *Education should be gradual and progressive.** Dr. Mayo states and explains this principle as follows : —*Development should be essen-*

its means of development from the circumstances of life ; methods of teaching and governing should not be confined to one artificial system ; and teachers should not push any rule or principle to excess, or use it when not applicable. Thus, because it is recommended to exercise the minds of children on visible objects, from their suitableness to the first stage of children, it is not to be supposed that everything is to be taught by objects, or the children confined to subjects about which discoveries can be made by the exercise of their senses. The subjects of instruction should be sufficiently numerous to secure the exercise of all the intellectual faculties, furnish with general information, and fit for all the duties of society ; objects should be presented, both natural and artificial, with their qualities, circumstances of place, number, &c., their history, actions, uses, &c., in order to cultivate observation ; past events, texts, hymns, tables, facts in geography, and definitions and rules in grammar, &c., should be learnt, in order to cultivate memory ; the judgment and reasoning powers should be exercised in their earliest stages on the objects, actions, qualities, and operations which the children daily examine ; direct instructions should be followed by study, and the instructor converted into an examiner and supplementer of the child's acquisitions ; children should be carried rapidly over some subjects of instruction in order to develop power and energy, and slowly over others in order to give habits of minute investigation.

* This principle arises out of the organic character of education ; all that is organic grows, *i.e.*, naturally and progressively unfolds itself ; therefore education should be gradual and progressive. It is also founded on the fact that the faculties of children are gradually exercised in strength and ability ; and we must follow

tially progressive.—The *sentiments* should be gradually led to take a higher direction and a wider range. The *motives* of well-doing must be by degrees elevated and purified in their character; the *duty* which was discharged at first in obedience to an earthly father must be set forth as the requirement of a heavenly one; the *charities of life* must be exercised towards those in immediate contact; by degrees an interest may be cultivated in operations embracing a wider or distant sphere of usefulness.*

the progress of nature. The principle might be fully stated thus— That as the minds of children, like their bodies, develop and come to maturity step by step, education, in order to follow nature, should be progressive and gradual, keeping pace with the development of the faculties; and should be united in its parts like a chain whose links form a continuous series. It is beautiful to observe how perfectly this principle is in harmony with all around. Gradual progress marks all that we see, both in nature and society. It is worthy of remark that the idea of graduating education is not new. Paulus Æginata, a Greek of the sixth or seventh century, laid down a graduated course of education founded on the laws of the periodic growth of children. This view, however, was first introduced in recent times, and practically carried out by Pestalozzi.

* The progressive character of the Pestalozzian system may be applied in the progression (1) of ideas; (2) of instruction or study; (3) of the development of the faculties; (4) of the moral treatment of children. The moral feelings should not only take a direction to higher objects at last culminating in God, and a range embracing the most distant relations and duties, but there should be the

" The cultivation of the higher intellectual faculties of judgment, reason, and taste is preceded by the careful development of just observation, clear intellectual conception, and accurate generalization. For this purpose real objects are presented to the examination of the younger pupils; the physical

graduation of a successive development and exercise. The moral nature of a child does not develop in all its parts at the same period. Some feelings are in operation much earlier than others, and consequently should be acted on first. Some are active and almost as vigorous in the child as in the full-grown man, as the desire of action, curiosity, sympathy, imitativeness, faith, and love of approbation; whilst caution, a sense of self-importance, reverence, the sense of the beautiful, and conscience, are of a later development. In the moral treatment of children at different stages regard must be paid to this fact. In order to secure the permanent possession of right feelings and the practice of right conduct; to work the springs of moral character, and even to administer punishment justly and effectively, to check a disposition or subdue the will, there must be much discriminating gradation of procedure. Take the following examples, and they will be found to succeed each other, and thus form a succession, if not a true gradation. 1st. *Exhibit* right conduct and feeling; 2nd. *Express* right feelings and views; 3rd. *Inculcate* and explain right feelings and practices; 4th. *Lead* the children to indulge in right feelings and to practise right conduct. The first is the simplest, and appeals to sympathy and imitativeness; the second, to faith and habit, which are both strong in children; the third, to the understanding and the relations of things which call forth the judgment; and the fourth, to various principles of action under the influence of the will—the most advanced.

Nothing exhibits gradation more clearly than the principles of senses are trained to accurate perception, full descriptions are given to call forth apprehension, and the understanding is gradually led to generalize and classify the notices it receives through them." Else-

action by which children are influenced; a wise teacher will, therefore, be careful to follow their development. Nature first develops the mechanical, consisting of instinct and habit, and for a time these predominate. No real motives to action exist, and the judicious mother or teacher throws herself upon the power of habit, trusts to instinct, and thus carries forward the work of education. Next are developed the animal principles of action, and the child is stimulated accordingly. And lastly, appear the rational principles of action, in which the noblest elements of man's nature are drawn out towards the Supreme Being, whose will and pleasure become the motive. The child is led to act as an intelligent and moral being, governed by reason and conscience and the will of God. .It is consequently at this period that appeals are made to the reason, that the sense of duty is called forth, and God made the supreme object of regard. The child is now prepared to act under the test of all government—self-government : and thus he arrives at the crowning-point of moral education. *For* this, the previous stages prepared ; *towards* this, the parent or teacher of intelligence continually looks forward ; and *at* this, the child arrives only when properly handled. But how many are all their lives mere creatures of habit, and of those instincts that we have in common with the lower animals? As to discipline, the practice of increasing punishments in duration or in kind until the disposition is eradicated or the will subdued is a painful example in point.

In early infancy the mental constitution presents the rudiments of those powers which characterize the human being in mature age. The several faculties of emotion and thought are essentially the same in the child as in the man, but some are developed much

where Dr. Mayo remarks, that "physical observation precedes physical conception, and physical
conceptions lead to metaphysical abstractions by
the intermediate link of general conceptions; and
in every branch of instruction a correct observation
of facts or data is placed before the process of judg-

sooner than others. Observation or perception is the first that
opens in the human mind, appearing before conception, and conception before judgment. The association of ideas takes place
sooner than memory ; and afterwards comes to the aid of the latter
faculty, Judgment respecting ideas of objects and actions appears
sooner than that of moral ideas. Ideality, simple abstraction, and
intuitive reason are developed at a comparatively early period ;
whereas complex abstraction and abstract reason are the latest
in the development of the human mind. Again, observation,
simple memory, and the dramatic element of imagination are
almost as vigorous in the child as they are in the full-grown man,
whilst philosophical memory, imagination, abstraction, and reason
do not gain vigour before a comparatively mature state of mind.

Even in the same faculty its various functions are not performed
equally early. In *judgment*, for example, the sense of *resemblance*
with respect to the visible and tangible forms of things comes before
the power of discriminating *differences ;* hence children apply the
names of individuals to species, and the names of species to genera,
long before they analyze and classify. Again, differences are
noticed before the sense of ratio is in any degree of activity—that
sense which is chiefly concerned with the circumstances, sequence,
or order of proportion and dependence. Further, the transition
is gradual from the discernment of resemblance to the more active
perception of analogy, which relates to what is more abstruse, in-
volving identity of principle or mode of action or construction as
well as sameness in use or final cause.

ing or reasoning upon them. Realities should also precede signs; and of signs, those which are significant by nature take the priority of those which are significant by compact."

Intellectual exercises, which are given at the usual lessons, should be so graduated, that one step would prepare for the next, and supply the pupils with a reason for taking it. "But," says Dr. Mayo, " in the ordinary methods of teaching, the course of instruction is founded on *abstract scientific considerations of the knowledge to be conveyed.* In the Pestalozzian method, the course is arranged on *psychological principles, derived from the consideration of the nature and position of the beings to be instructed.* In every branch of study the *point de départ* is sought in the actual experience of the child; and from that point where he intellectually is, he is progressively led to that point where the instructor wishes him to be. Thus he proceeds from the *known* to the *unknown*, by a process that connects the latter with the former; and, instead of being abruptly placed in contact with the abstract elements of a science, he is led by a course of analytical investigations of the knowledge actually possessed to form for himself those intellectual abstractions which are in general presented as the primary truths. Thus a *natural* development

founded on *particulars*, varying in some circumstances, precedes and prepares for the *artificial*
development, founded on *general*, invariable
truth." *

* In the progress of study the child proceeds from the natural
signs of looks and gestures to the conventional tones of the mother
tongue—from living sounds in language to dead characters in
books, and from reality in the object-lesson to the signs of it printed
in the description.   Speech precedes reading, as reading is
followed by writing. Objects precede pictures, which are used
antecedently to maps, diagrams, and other artificial representations.
The contemplations of deeds, whether of faith and love, or otherwise, go before conceptions and the descriptions of them couched
in terms and definitions.   In arithmetic, the child proceeds from
ideas of number in connection with objects, to mental calculations,
where he still comes face to face with numbers themselves, though
not with the bodily, but with the mental eye.   From these he passes
to ciphering, where the numbers are seen through symbols.   In
like manner the child proceeds from examples and particular ideas
to general descriptions, definitions, and rules, as in grammar and
number ; in natural phenomena, from the particular phenomenon
occurring under the child's observation to the general law by which
it is regulated ; in form or geometry, from descriptions of particular
solids to that of general resemblances, ending in abstract conceptions ; in the study of the human heart, from observing the
manifestations in himself and others to reading the lives of great
men, and from that to those of mankind in the pages of history.
Even writing and reading are good examples of a gradual procedure.
The teacher analyzes these into their elements, teaches the latter in
succession, and then combines them by a process of synthetic
teaching.   In writing taught after the method of Malhauser, and
the Phonic method of teaching to read, practised in the schools of
the Institution, we have additional specimens of a gradual pro-

"A connected course in intellectual education not only facilitates the acquisition of knowledge,

cedure. But, perhaps, in the graduated course of instruction drawn up for the infant schools of this Institution there is the best · specimen of a careful graduation of subjects of elementary instruction that has emanated from the school of Pestalozzi. In teaching "*Colour*," six steps are carefully followed.—1st, distinguishing colours ; 2nd, naming colours ; 3rd, distinguishing shades of colour ; 4th, naming and arranging shades of colours ; 5th, exercising the conceptive powers in describing colours and shades of colours; 6th, the judgment of colour in the formation of secondary colours, &c., their mixture, &c. In lessons on "*Form*," the 1st step is that of distinguishing regular forms; 2nd, the parts of forms ; 3rd, names or phrases indicative of name ; 4th, comparison of forms ; 5th, solids of a regular character observed, named, and described ; 6th, classification of forms ; 7th, with elder children, lines and angles as matters of observation, judgment, and reasoning ; 8th, geometry. In lessons on "*Sound*" the 1st step is to distinguish common sound ; the 2nd, to imitate the same ; the 3rd, to distinguish and imitate musical sounds as to length ; the 4th, as to pitch ; 5th, as to volume ; 6th, musical notation ; 7th, combination of elements, with applications to singing, differing in degrees of complexity ; the 8th, vocal music. The ease and pleasure alike of teaching and learning, when graduation is thus practically carried out, may be witnessed in any Pestalozzian school. All the elementary subjects of instruction have been carefully graduated in our own schools, as may be seen by consulting the manuals of the Society. Simplification can only be carried too far, and continued too long, when the mind becomes so accustomed to receive knowledge divided into its most simple elements that it is not prepared to embrace complicated ideas, or to make those rapid strides in investigation and conclusion which is one of the most important results of a sound education.

O

but shows the relation in which different truths stand to each other." *

* In addition to these advantages of a progressive method of proceeding, acquisition proceeds more steadily, the children are made happier, smiles take the place of sighs, the teacher proceeds with more ease, certainty, and satisfaction.   2nd, rote learning is avoided, that error of teachers who allege that such and such subjects must be learnt merely, as they cannot be understood ; whereas by beginning a little lower, and by waiting a little until the faculties were further developed, they would substitute intelligence and pleasure for jargon and disgust.   The progress of a child both intellectually and morally is like ascending a ladder ; when he attempts to take two steps at a time he runs the risk of falling to the bottom.   Hence his footing should always be made firm on one step .before he is led to the next.   Proceeding thus he may ultimately be led to any height.   The beauty as well as the benefit of the progressive perfection of the human soul is very great, and the benevolent designs of the Supreme Being therein conspicuous. He does all things well.   Here nature acts slowly, gradually, and well, without crowding or hurrying.

Again, *progressive* advancement stands in opposition to the haste and blind groping of many teachers without system.   It endeavours to find the proper point of commencing, and to proceed in a slow and gradual, but uninterrupted course, always waiting until the first point should have a certain degree of distinctness in the mind of the child, before entering upon the exhibition of the second.   In fact, the intellectual exercises will thus be so graduated that one step prepares the way for the next, and prepares the pupil with a reason for taking it.   The advantages of a right starting-point and regular gradation have been proved to be incalculable.   Look at the application of this principle in changing the character of the instruction given both in the infant schools of the poor and the nurseries of the rich.   For geometry, "form and size" are

Dr. Mayo adds in his Introduction to "Lessons on Shells :"—"*Every age has its intellectual as well as its moral claims,* and though the stern discipline of early classical instruction may offer some advantages, still the hours devoted to the abstractions of grammar, and the puzzling out ideas which have no prototype in the child's mind through the dark mist of a language little akin to his maternal tongue, present very meagre food to that understanding they are supposed to strengthen. If the child must lisp in Latin, let him do so; let his first 'Gradus ad Parnassum' be through the quagmires at its base; the few choice spirits that mount the summit may, perhaps, tread it with firmer step, and enjoy the prospect with

substituted; for arithmetic, "number;" for geography, "place;" for mechanics, "weight," and so forth. Why? Because they are elementary, and appeal to the senses. The effect produced in older schools, if the principle were intelligently and thoroughly applied, would be still greater. Sensuous instruction would be admitted more largely. Isolated facts would be introduced before attempts were made at connected reasoning on them. Correct speaking would be attended to before correct grammar. The judgments and reasonings of authors would not be forced on the mere memory. Generalities and abstractions, as put at the beginning of school-books, would be placed at the end. Attempts at the cultivation of taste, especially in connection with the imagination, would not be made until the pupil had attained greater intellectual stature. There would be no precocious, unhealthy development. Let teachers deal with the faculties as they come to their hand, and they will find that they will ultimately be amply rewarded.

keener relish ; but that step will not be the less firm,
nor that relish the less keen, because a daily hour was
abstracted for 'Lessons on Objects,' or 'Lessons on
Shells.' Not only are the sciences so linked together
that each gives each a double charm, but the faculties
of the mind are so constituted, as that the vigour
of each is promoted by the due development of the
rest. And there is a harmony as truly existing in
a properly educated mind as in a well-formed and
well-exercised body, though the harmony of the
former may not be so easily discerned as that of the
latter." Again, " As every age *has its intellectual
claims*, so also has *every grade of talent.* The schools
of the highest reputation have generally been conducted too exclusively to the advantage of the
superior class of minds. The fine porcelain has been
beautifully moulded and delicately pencilled, but the
coarser clay has been almost entirely neglected. Yet
many a young man who will never shine in the Senate
House or the schools may yet pursue natural history
with success, and find in such pursuits improvement
for his mind, a refuge from *ennui*, and a substitute
for sensual pleasures. There is much truth, as well
as benevolence, in a remark I once heard from an
amiable coadjutor of Pestalozzi, ' *Tout terrain est bon
si l'on sait le cultiver.*' "

But there should not only be progressive development of the faculties, but progressive instruction according with the gradually expanding nature of the children.

"There is a certain order," says Dr. Mayo, "in which truths present themselves to the mind engaged in the original investigation of a subject, and when the subject has been investigated, a different arrangement is necessary for the lucid expositions of the truths discovered. These views have been most unhappily applied in the early stages of instruction. For, although the artificial order may be best calculated to convey knowledge to minds already trained for its reception by previous acquaintance with similar subjects, it is by no means suited to the opening faculties of children. Hence the disgust, in many cases insurmountable, which the first principles of a science inspire in their minds. This disgust, however, vanishes, if a preparatory course of instruction be arranged, having for its object the training the mind for the study of the science rather than the communicating the knowledge of it. In this preparatory course the order is determined by a consideration of the mind of the pupil; it commences with what is already known to him, and proceeds to the proximate truth; the more easy precedes the more difficult; the individual prepares for the general truth; the example for the rule."

In his Introduction to the Cheam Grammar, Dr. Mayo makes the following remarks, which, whilst more immediately concerned with the teaching of language, further illustrate the principle of proceeding gradually with the young, whether in relation to knowledge or the development of the mind. Although they refer to the acquisition of the classics, they may also be turned to account in teaching the mother tongue.

"In spite of every indication which the youthful mind spontaneously gives, that it is led from the perception of particular truths to the conception of universal propositions—that it must first see embodied in realities and clothed with circumstances the ideas which it is afterwards to recognize in their pure, abstract, intellectual form — the prevailing practice is forcibly to drive a child of tender years through the generalities of grammar, unintelligible and uninteresting to him, till at last, in the course of their application in practice, the true order of thought is established in his mind, and he understands and appreciates his grammar through the knowledge which he derives from studying the language itself. The objections to this course are so obvious that it is not to be wondered at that a variety of plans of instruction should have been formed on principles diametrically opposite. By means of translation, oral or printed, free or literal, interlinear or interpaged, with various degrees of ingenuity, they have carried the self-complacent pupil along their easy declivities, cramming him with an ill-digested knowledge of the literature of the language, and leaving the grammar to 'toil after them in vain,' a kind of '*pœna pede claudo.*' But this is a mistake. To attain the end we have in view, and rightly to fix the knowledge we would communicate, we must attach the same importance to grammatical instruction that has been assigned to it in our ancient institutions; accurate knowledge and ready application of its forms and principles must be made the predominant feature, the never-forgotten aim of early lessons : '*Hinc spes roboris.*' But these forms and principles should first be traced in analyzing passages of ancient authors, selected for the purpose of exhibiting them. In this manner the value and use of grammatical knowledge will be felt in the acquiring it, and a much clearer conception of its principles will be formed. But the committing to memory the result of this observation, as it is presented in the grammar itself, must follow step by step, and not be reserved altogether for a later period. It is not necessary that each particular form should be seen in some selected passage before it is read in the grammar; the end is answered if some prominent points are thus presented.

"The grammar may be referred to as supplying a complete as well as a systematic arrangement. In such a course as this, previous observation and analysis give life to the grammar, and the grammar committed to memory gives solidity, permanency, and order to the knowledge practically acquired. Thus the positive knowledge sought is effectually attained, and the faculties of the pupil are bene ficially exercised in attaining it. His mind is con sequently improved in a higher degree, and more real progress is made than would have been the case, *cæteris paribus*, under either of the rival modes of in struction.

"The principle here laid down is susceptible of various modifications in its practical application, and it has, in fact, been applied in various manners in the Institution of Pestalozzi himself and elsewhere. All that, strictly speaking, I contend for is the principle itself—the mode of reducing it to practice I leave to the discretion of the teacher."

Principle 8.—Education ought to be free and natural, instead of being cramped, confined, and servile. *

---

* Pestalozzi laid it down as a principle that education should be adapted to individual character and not to children in a mass—that it ought to be "free and natural, instead of being cramped, confined, servile," running in a groove or channel, and attempting to

mould all minds into one general form. He held that the mind should not only have sufficient liberty to manifest its individual character, but that the cultivation or treatment should, as far as possible, be adapted to the individual character. For this purpose he required close attention to be paid by the teacher to the peculiarities of every child, and of each sex, in order that he might acquire the development and qualifications necessary for the situation to which the Creator destined him, and be prepared to labour successfully for those among whom he was placed.

It is well to view children in their points of resemblance, in order to adapt their treatment and teaching to the general principles of their nature ; but their education cannot be carried on effectually without noticing their individual distinctiveness. It is here that the study of character is necessary, and helps to give certainty to all our proceedings. By this study the mental chemist (so to speak) can tell the constituents of his soil, as well as the agricultural chemist, like him, point out what is redundant and what is defective, and act accordingly. The "sympathy of numbers," though a truth, is but a partial one, and when used indiscriminately belongs to that species of quackery that would apply a special remedy as a universal recipe. The influence of numbers united with the spirit that sanctifies a virtuous home is good, but it is a principle that applies more to moral than intellectual education. True, "the sympathy of numbers" may be brought into operation at gallery instruction, and a teacher can thus give instruction to a large number at once, and thereby economize teaching power. But is the teaching as efficient as if the gallery were broken up into two or three classes ? Is not the individuality of the children sunk in the mass, and all measured by the same rule ?

Pestalozzi would never sanction the teaching or training of children in large numbers on one uniform plan. The class was his standard, and even there he would adapt himself to the particular dispositions and characters of the children. Like the principles already taken up, this has its origin in the laws of the human mind, of which Pestalozzi was a diligent student, and on which his whole system is founded. It is an obvious and a well-established fact in mental science, confirmed by daily observation and experience, that the different faculties of the human soul are possessed of very different degrees of endowment or natural force in different individuals, and that in the same individual they vary in their degree of power ; some being weak and some strong, whilst others occupy a medium position.

It is this which gives rise to those peculiarities by which every mind is marked, and to the endless varieties in the character and tastes of individuals, and consequently in their pursuits. It is this which gives rise to what is termed the predisposition, or bias, of the individual, and constitutes what has been called his idiosyncrasies.

The diversities of character are twofold, intellectual and moral. These diversities must be met and treated with discrimination and care. In one child *memory* takes the lead, and, as it were, throws into the shade all the other powers of the mind. Such a one must first have collected everything in his storehouse before he can elaborate it. In another, almost everything comes through *imagination*. He envinces little or no reason, but carefully marks such narratives as come under his notice, and makes whatever pleases him in them his own. He writes correct orthography, and yet he does not know a single orthographical rule. Another pursues quite an opposite course. His *judgment* approves, and it is only what he thus approves that he treasures up. His magazine, if we may so speak, is poorer ; but his store has been selected after his own fashion. All his mental possessions are carefully selected and laboriously acquired. Some excel in the exercise of the reflective powers, by which they ascertain premises, deduce inferences, and draw conclusions. In a word, they have the logical faculty, which is always tracing to causes or consequences. Then there is the mechanical genius, who, though he seems to effect little or nothing in the school, will probably become as an artisan much more useful than his neighbour, who, though of much quicker parts, will probably make a worse workman, not possessing sufficient patience and steadiness for labours of a mechanical kind. Again, there is the embryo artist who sketches all sorts of things in his book or on the walls, and amongst the rest a baby brother or sister's face. In such a one we may see a future Landseer or a West. Who would attempt to teach and deal with all these diversities of intellectual character in the same way, if they are to be improved?

From the neglect of this important principle much time is wasted in school by fruitless efforts to pursue courses for which nature has not qualified the pupil. Let the hours spent in music by those who have no ear—upon drawing by those who might almost be said to have no eye—upon languages by those who never afterwards speak any but their mother tongue, be added together, year after year, and an aggregate of wasted time will present itself sufficient to alarm those who are sensible of its value, and of the responsibility of using it aright.

As to moral character or dispositions, these diversities are very numerous. In the boy who always manages to be the driver of what he calls his horses, or the girl who is the directress at games and the patroness and guide of the younger ones, the love of power is at work. Again, a child who separates from companions, and is found musing often, with a smile now and then playing over the face, is imaginative and solitary, living in his own land of dreams. One child is timid and needs encouragement ; another, pert and bold, requiring to be repressed. One child is prone to pleasure, another to carelessness, and a third to presumption. One can be ruled only by fear, while another must be guided by love. Further, moral diversities exhibit an unvarying combination of certain definite virtues with certain definite vices. One is open-hearted and generous, but self-willed, headstrong, and forward ; another is quiet and patient, but reserved, sulky, and revengeful ; a third is gentle and amiable, but with a morbid sensibility that will lead to a thousand future wounds ; a fourth is bold and fearless, but proud and domineering.

Principle 9.—*Education should be based on intuition ;* and particularly the right basis of elementary instruction Pestalozzi maintained to be intuition.*

Religiously, the same differences exist, following the same variety
of temperament. What may be the primal cause of these differences,
whether wholly in natural constitution, wholly in early influences,
or partly in both, is a speculation into which we have no occasion
to enter. We take their existence as a confessed fact, and we contend that it demands, as essential to efficient education, a corresponding personal influence which shall discriminate in each case its
particular dangers and deficiencies, and be suited to the wants of
each pupil. It is certain that a mode of treatment effectual for one
would be ruinous for another, and the moral medicine of one be the
moral poison of another. Each pupil must be dealt with under a
common classification, with such modifications as an individual
influence over each can alone render possible. To one, the terrors
of the Lord ; to another, the gentleness of the Saviour, must be
exhibited, as it is infallibly declared by God Himself : " Of some
have compassion, making a difference, and others save with fear,
pulling them out of the fire, hating even the garments spotted by
the flesh."

In both instruction and discipline these diversities or modifications
render the strictest attention on the part of the teacher necessary ;
and prove that simultaneous teaching and one mode of treatment
are incompatible with the nature of the case.

* There is a constant use of this term in the present day, and
round it is waged the fiercest of disputes both in the domain of
philosophy and theology. We need not, therefore, wonder at its
introduction into education, and its being made the battle-ground of
a system. For a clear understanding of the subject, it will be
necessary to look at the different applications of the term, to ascer-

tain how the founder of our system applied it, and how far it has been admitted into our English Pestalozzianism.

In the common acceptation of the term, intuition denotes the act of the mind in perceiving truth without argument, testimony, or experience. The truth is arrived at by spontaneous suggestion, and the process is the same as instinct. In this sense intuitive and instinctive are equivalent. Thus, whenever any idea comes into play in the mind independently of any conscious effort, it is said to be intuitive. Intuition is higher in degree than instinct, the character of the human spirit being higher and more complex than that of the brute. In this sense all the faculties and powers, the passions and emotions of the human soul, are intuitive. In what may be called the theological sense, intuition is used as synonymous with "consciousness," "common sense," "first principles," "self-evident truths," "natural knowledge," "fundamental reason," "light of reason," "light of conscience," "inward Divine light." In this sense it is not so much to any distinct mental faculty as to the mind itself, with all its powers, that reference is made. It exists as a mere capacity independent of experience for the first occasion of its action, and upon successive experiences for its gradual development and culture. It constitutes what is called the verifying power or faculty by which the truth or falsehood of whatever is presented to the mind can be decided. There are those who hold that by means of this power man is a sufficient guide to himself; and, instead of needing to be enlightened by the Bible, is qualified to sit in judgment on the Bible, and by "feeling, or inspiration, to see the truth at once and without any intervening medium," even that of Revelation. This is intuitional theology, or German Rationalism.

McCosh, in his "Intuitions of the Mind," and Tate, in his "Philosophy of Education," use the term in its philosophical or higher educational sense. They apply the term to the various powers of the mind. The former writer says that the mind of man has a set of simple cognitive powers from which we obtain our primitive cognitions. It has also a set of reproductive powers by which it recalls the past in old forms produced by memory, or in new dispositions produced by imagination. The mind has also a power of comparison by which it perceives relations and forms judgments that are primitive or intuitional when simple and obvious. Hence it is that Tate speaks of intuitive observation, intuitive conception, intuitive memory, intuitive judgment, and intuitive reason, as distinct from the developed, conscious, and complex exercise of these various faculties, especially when under the guidance of experience and the power of abstraction. But all this seems to indicate a step in the development of these several faculties rather than a distinct power.

In the note on pp. 33—35 is given what may be called the Pestalozzian acceptation of the term intuition. By it Pestalozzi understood the impression received by the external senses, communicated directly to the mind, and by which it obtains the consciousness of any object. It is thus with regard to a large class of subjects synonymous with observation or perception in the English sense. When Pestalozzi speaks of intuitive perception, he means sensuous perception as distinguished from the perception of the understanding or simple apprehension and judgment. But when Pestalozzi pursued the subject of education to a more advanced age in the child, he spoke likewise of mental, moral, and religious intuition; that is, of a perception of the understanding, the moral feelings, and the religious faculties of man. The ideas derived from those sources he regarded as distinct from all information derived from outward sources, inasmuch as they rest on internal consciousness. And he would base the intellectual, moral, and religious education of the child upon intuition equally with physical perception. It is here that this Institution parts company with Pestalozzi, and would cordially join in the sentiments expressed by Miss Mayo at p. 46, and the note appended at p. 49. At the same time we know that his practice was far better than his principles. It was said that he attached little importance to testimony as one of the sources of our knowledge, and devoted too little attention to historical truth. But he never questioned Divine testimony as given in the sacred records, nor neglected Bible teaching. Indeed, the great leader and expounder of the Bible and religious truth at Yverdon was Niederer, an Evangelical clergyman of the Swiss Protestant Church.

It has also been said that " Pestalozzi was accustomed to observe that history was but a 'tissue of lies,' and forgot that it is necessary to occupy the pupil with man and with moral events as well as with nature and matter, if we wish to cultivate properly his moral powers and elevate him above the material world." But we believe that this was more from accident, and the circumstances of education at the time, than from premeditated choice. Deficiency and extravagance have been charged against ourselves in this place. Our system has been called the "no-telling system ; " because we devote much attention to subjects of instruction that can be acquired by the children themselves by observation and reflection in connection with a system of questioning. At one time books were thought to be ignored by this Institution, because from the character of the methods pursued instruction was very largely given orally, and thus the minds of the pupils brought into greater activity.

It is rather in the extent of the operations of intuition that we disclaim, or at least doubt, Pestalozzi. With McCosh, we "would as soon believe that there are no such agents as heat, chemical affinity, and electricity in physical nature as that there are no immediate perceptions and native-born convictions in this mind of ours." The most accurate and most practical view for the teacher to take of intuition is, that it forms one of the original powers by which thought is created, one of the six sources from which, or channels through which, knowledge reaches the mind. For an account of these channels see "Child and Book," under the head of "Origin of Ideas," pp. 94—97 ; where an accurate view of both the extent and the limits of this important faculty is given. The teacher ought to be able to make discriminating use of it in education,

Principle 10.—*Education should be analytical;* everything taught should be first reduced to its elements. It is an essential feature of the system of Pestalozzi that the teachers should analyze and find the simplest elements of the knowledge to be acquired, and then, leading the pupil to an acquaintance with these, enable him to build up by his own exertion the edifice of learning, and make it completely his own. Thus the first task of the Pestalozzian instructor is analytic, that of the children synthetic; the latter begin at the lowest point, and ultimately reach the highest—they begin with the elements, then combine them.*

and turn it to the highest account. He will avoid mistakes by remembering that in the spheres of morality and religion, as well as in that of the intellect, intuition has only to do with ideas, and only indicates a means of acquisition, and that a limited one.

* If Pestalozzi had done no more for early education than reduce different branches of knowledge to their elements, and thereby simplify the subjects, find a right starting-point for the child's career in the acquisition of knowledge, and secure a more intelligent attention and interest, he would have been a benefactor to the infantine class. What Baron Liebig has done for practical purposes, Pestalozzi did for practical education. The Russian Government conferred a diploma of honour on the Baron for the application of his theoretical knowledge of chemistry to the practical purposes of life; in like manner should the memory of Pestalozzi be embalmed for applying the theories of mental philosophy to the

Such is Pestalozzianism as developed by Pestalozzi himself, and by individuals who gave to Pestalozzi his just meed of credit, as the originator of the system. The result of the application of these principles is clearly pointed out by Dr. Mayo : — " A pupil educated thus in harmony with his own nature feels an interest in his studies unknown to those who are subjected to an unnatural process ; and the genuine metaphysical experiences, which he insensibly treasures up, supply him with invaluable advantages for self-knowledge and self-improvement in after life. Whatever application, distortion, or mutilation of these principles may be practically made by those who profess to adopt them, they must recommend themselves to the Christian parent, as a faithful reflection of the light of the Gospel : for *the method of Pestalozzi is, in its essence, the application of Christianity to the business of education.*"

practice of the schoolroom. As is so common, however, in all discoveries, his analysis was imperfect. Language, Number, and Form are not the whole of the elements of instruction. Indeed, Language, whilst a distinct and important part, is not an element at all. What, however, was but imperfectly done by Pestalozzi has been completed by the Home and Colonial School Society. And not only so, but these elements have been worked out into a graduated series of lessons, carrying the infant through all the stages of intuitive development, and bringing him up to the usual complex branches of instruction taught in the juvenile school.

We might extend our quotations by drawing upon writers of another class—educators who speak in Pestalozzian phrase, and evidently borrow from Pestalozzian sources, but have not acknowledged their obligations. But we forbear.

THE METHODS OF PESTALOZZI.

It remains only to make a few concluding remarks on the method of Pestalozzi. We have already mentioned the comprehensive view he took of education ; that he considered whatever God bestowed on man was a talent to be cultivated ; that he took nature as his guide, and commenced the work with those faculties which first appear, carefully watching the dawn of each power, carefully preserving a due equipoise between them, endeavouring thus to carry on a harmonious and progressive development. We will, however, in concluding, enter a little more into detail. And first as to instruction :—

The object of Pestalozzi was to collect all the elementary means of developing the faculties by the most natural processes. The first materials are supplied by the impressions the child receives from the external world. The crowd of objects that present themselves to his observation causes at first a real chaos in his mind, but, insensibly, the impressions produced by the things continually before him acquire more distinctness; next arises the desire of communicating to others what he experiences himself; the organ of speech is not then long before it performs its office. With the assistance of language, sensations acquire day by day more precision. But all this forms only the basis of the column. Impressions thus received prepare the way for higher mental exercises. Soon the presence of the object is not necessary to call forth the idea—by a simple act of his will, his imagination reproduces it—his memory recalls it—he sees it with the eyes of his mind — he can retrace its form — determine its proportions; he compares, judges, reasons; and the little being, so lately inferior to the brutes in intelligence, manifests the distinguishing characteristics of man. Such is the course of nature; Pestalozzi took it as his guide; he was convinced from what he observed, first, that the intellectual faculties of a child only require to be developed carefully, gradually, and steadily, to elevate him to the highest point to which man can attain; and, secondly, that the little success hitherto obtained in education ought to be attributed to the weakness and incoherence of the foundation upon which different systems had been based; and especially to the little care taken to give to the impressions received in infancy a direction conformable to the indications furnished by nature. Pestalozzi sought to discover the most simple means of giving the child this direction, so that the teaching of art might harmonize and co-operate with that of nature.

After a long series of observations and experiments, he came to the conclusion, that the first distinct ideas called out in a child by exterior objects were the result of observations that he made naturally on their *form* and their *number*, combined with the knowledge he had acquired of their *name*. In consequence, he proposed an elementary course of instruction consisting of three branches. The first embraced the intuitive perception of the objects of nature and art by which the child is surrounded, with the acquisition of their names, and to this he gave the name of *language*. The second embraced intuitive instruction in *number*. The third, intuitive instruction with respect to *form* and *dimensions*.

1. *Language.*—With respect to the first branch of instruction, Pestalozzi arranged a course comprising five steps.

In the *first step* the child is taught to distinguish the sounds of language, and imitate them. It contained a complete series of articulate sounds, which the child is to repeat sometimes slowly, sometimes quickly, but always distinctly; the mother sometimes singing them, varying the tone and expression.

In the *second step* the child learns to name every-thing brought under his notice, without any order or arrangement, taking advantage of whatever creates a want or excites curiosity. From naming things he proceeds to distinguish and to learn how to speak of their various properties, and thus gradually acquires an abundant supply of words, with which he also connects clear ideas.

The object in the *third step* is to lead the child to fix his attention successively on whatever in any object naturally calls out his observation. He will learn to distinguish and name the different parts and most striking qualities of an animal, a plant, or a stone, and thus the habit is formed of observing with intelligence everything around him, and the power acquired of expressing himself correctly with respect to them.

At the *fourth step* it is proposed to lead the child to perceive the points of difference in the objects of which he has observed the principal characteristics; thus, that the horse is a quadruped with an undivided hoof; the ox, a quadruped with a cloven hoof; that the willow is a tree with pointed leaves; the oak a tree with jagged leaves, &c.

The *fifth step*—the difference observed in the pre-ceding steps becomes the basis of the instruction proposed in this. The child is to be exercised in arranging in one row all objects of a similar nature·

These lessons not only embrace a knowledge of qualities, but are extended to actions and uses; and this leads to a large sphere of instruction—to the terms used in arts and in natural history, in trades and occupations. With respect to actions, the child may be exercised in determining their object, utility, danger, &c.; he may be led to observe the following or other circumstances, and to express himself with relation to them, *viz.*, What usually performs such an action? When is it done? Where is it done? Why is it done? How is it done? What good is it? What harm?

In this way the child may be exercised in acquiring positive ideas of a number of things that might otherwise strike his eyes, but not arouse his intelligence. One benefit arising from such instruction is the learning to associate the name with the thing signified, and the name calls up the idea of what it stands for. In this way the habit of viewing the material world with intelligence is cultivated, excited, and this combined with the power of correct and ready expression. A great difficulty, and one that impedes every instant those engaged in teaching the children of the poorer classes, is that of making themselves understood. Things, even the most simple, require long definitions, and then, after all, fail to make the matter intelligible to the pupil, who, in fact, has no just idea of the true meaning of terms in which they are expressed.

Further, he is prepared to enter upon the abstractions and generalizations of grammar ; for particular facts and truths lead to the conception of general propositions. "The general ideas which, in the science of grammar, are presented as abstractions, he has seen embodied in realities, and clothed with circumstances : his course has been from the concrete to the abstract, from the particular to the general, from the example to the rule ; and this is the natural course." Pestalozzi addresses his instructions in the first rudiments of language to mothers, with whom should commence the task of cultivating the faculty of speech, and calls upon them most earnestly and affectionately to do their duty fully by their offspring. Our trained teachers, however, often conduct this subject efficiently upon the models set in our manuals of instruction. At this elementary stage of his course, the teaching of Pestalozzi was chiefly oral and catechetical, illustrated as much as possible by natural objects and by demonstration. Books were not resorted to till the mind of the child was in a state of healthy activity, awakened to a lively interest in truth, and arriving at it by inductive processes. As the higher faculties unfolded, the subjects presented were such as promoted their exercise and improvement. The instruction given had always a reference to the mind of the child : it was not the value of the acquisition to be made which was so much to be considered, as its effect in developing and strengthening the innate powers.*

2. *Number.*—The second elementary means by which Pestalozzi sought the development of the mental faculties was *number*. This at first he treated as a process of intuition, requiring that

---

* " A want of order and arrangement in the original lessons on objects has been alleged as a blemish ; exercises so miscellaneous in their character, so devoid of systematic arrangement, *were* regarded as essentially defective as means of intellectual development. Upon these grounds the miscellaneous object-lessons were abandoned even in the school of Pestalozzi, the master who conducted the class substituting a course on the parts and functions of the bodily frame. But this was a mistake ; the desultory character attaching to them in their original form is corrected in our English schools by making a previous selection of subjects and presenting them in the class-room. In point of fact, their miscellaneous character is a studied feature, as better suited to the intellectual state of the pupils. Their first steps should be the examination of objects as nature presents them, or rather, as they see them in nature ; that is, either as insulated or associated only by accidental connection. When ideas are formed and correct expressions familiarized, the business of classification commences, the lessons assume a more scientific character, and the pupils are prepared to enter on the province of natural history or any other natural science. Besides, as they are intended to be preparatory to instruction in natural history in all its departments, they gradually assume a more scientific character, and thus a feeling of progress is sustained in the pupil's mind. It has been found, indeed, by long experience, that no lessons produce more continued interest, or more enlarge the minds of children, than

before the abstract idea was presented to the child, he should perceive number connected with objects. Thus, the parts of his body may be used to give this idea; also stones, nuts, beads, &c. The instructor says to the child (not, Here is one), but, Here is one stone, one nut, &c.; and adding another, Here are two stones, two nuts, &c. When the child has thus been exercised in distinguishing and naming one, two, three—the different number of the objects presented —he will soon have an intuitive perception that the terms one, two, three, are always the same, whilst the objects to which they are applied vary; he will thus be prepared to separate the idea of number from that of the thing, and to ascend to the abstract idea. When he has a correct idea of the numbers up to ten, he is ready to carry on different combination of these numbers. By practical examples he learns to form rules for himself; he works his own way, acquiring power, vigour, and readiness at each advance: "he is not led hoodwinked through the intricacies of arithmetic," but understands what he is

those on objects. The training which lessons on objects will have supplied for commencing easy lessons on shells, or any other branch of natural history, will consist principally in the improved faculty of observing natural features, in the possession and command of a small vocabulary of scientific terms, in the habit of classification, and in the practice of giving a written summary of the knowledge acquired."—*Dr. Mayo.*

about, first becoming familiar with elements, and then enjoying the pleasure of finding the results of their various combinations. The whole is a reasonable exercise; he sees truth in all its processes, and his mind is trained to value intellectual as well as moral truth. There is harmony between the different branches of his education which is *felt*. Pestalozzi, in his course of arithmetic, excluded ciphers until the idea of numbers was perfectly understood, and the children had practice in the common operations mentally. The main object of his instruction was the development of the mental powers; and this he accomplished with so much success, that the ability his pupils displayed in mental arithmetic was one of the chief means of attracting the public attention to his experiment. *

* "The teaching of number at the earliest stages does not propose to explain processes, but to unfold principles. The pupil is not taught to comprehend a rule, but to dispense with it, or form it for himself. The path along which he is led may be longer than the usual route, but then it is in broad day-light; he is more independent of his guide, and derives more health and vigour from the exercise. Were the true ends of intellectual education more clearly apprehended, the means of prosecuting it would be more justly appreciated. While the question *Cui bono ?* so judicious in itself, is answered by a sordid reference to mere money-getting, or by a narrow-minded consideration of professional advancement, every method of instruction that proposes to itself a more exalted, though less obvious utility, will be ridiculed as visionary, or

3. *Form.*—The third branch of Pestalozzi's elementary instruction embraced *form* and its relations. It was similarly treated ; intuition was the basis of future acquisitions in knowledge.* The pupil gains from

neglected as unprofitable. But when the true end of intellectual education shall be admitted to be first the attainment of mental power, and then the application of it to practical and scientific purposes, that plan of early instruction which dwells long on first principles, and does not haste to make learned, will be acknowledged as the most economical, because the most effectual. Experience will show, as indeed it has already shown, that while superficial teaching may prepare for the mere routine of daily business, whensoever a question, not anticipated in the manual, occurs, none but the pupil whose faculties have been exercised in the investigation of truth, who is the master, not the slave of rules, will solve the unexpected difficulty by a novel application of the principles of the science."—*Dr. Mayo.*

* For a time intuition was not only the basis, but the superstructure, and in this we perceive the original and progressive character of the system of the great educator. We shall let Dr. Biber tell the story. '' As Pestalozzi was not aware of the existence of a mental intuition as clear and as certain as the intuition of the senses, he fell into the mistake common among reformers of all kinds ; in avoiding the extreme of mere nominal knowledge conveyed by the usual systems, he ran into an opposite one by keeping the child to the visible representations of number and form on outward objects, long beyond that period when they are conceived in the intellect as mental realities or ideas in the true sense of the word, and thus preventing the mind's emancipations from the external world. The merit of having pointed out this mistake is chiefly due to Niederer, who struggled against the tendency of Pestalozzi. The impulse which he gave produced very soon a

objects the ideas upon which he afterwards carries on the processes of reasoning : he learns the data of the science from the examination of geometrical solids : he deduces truth himself from facts he perceives to be true; and thus he gradually acquires the power of mathematical reasoning. Here, again, he works for himself—all is clear and real to him; and if the true end of education is to form the man, it is surely more likely to be effected by treating him as the agent rather than as the passive recipient. Under this system the child constructs his own edifice; his faculties are exercised in the investigation of truth, which is so presented that he arrives at it step by step, each advance preparing for the next. The great aim is the development of the precious germs folded up within his mind, and which, with expansion, acquire health and vigour. A child under such a system will, it is true, acquire less positive knowledge in a given number of years than one who has all communicated to him : but his knowledge will be his own; and he will have gained a mental independence and power which will

reform in the mathematical instruction of the establishment, and the pupils, after they had been allowed sufficient time by the aid of visible representations to acquire real ideas, were conducted to purely mental operations on the same subjects." This may account for some of the accusations brought against Pestalozzi, and at the same time form his vindication.

fit him for grappling with difficulties, and prepare him for whatever may be his position in life.

Under the head of Form Pestalozzi ranked writing, drawing, and geometry. The basis of each of these he considered to be the intuitive perception of form and its dimensions. Drawing, he thought, ought to be a universal acquirement, because the faculty for it is possessed by all, and because it would prove the means of leading the child from vague perceptions to clear ideas. He also considered that the art of measuring ought to precede that of drawing ; that is, that the eye should be practised in determining figure and proportion, before the hand is employed to execute these perceptions. If a child, he observes, is called upon to imitate objects or representations of objects before he has acquired a distinct notion of their proportions, his instructions in the art of drawing will fail to produce upon his mental development that beneficial influence which alone renders it worth learning. Writing, he maintained, should not be taught before, but after, drawing; and this also should be preceded by a previous proficiency in measuring lines ; for writing is, in fact, a sort of linear drawing, and that of fixed forms, from which no arbitrary or fanciful deviations are permitted. He also contended that the practice of writing when acquired previously to, and independently of, drawing, spoilt the hand and cramped its freedom, by confining it to a few peculiar forms. Another reason in favour of drawing being taught first was, he said, that by the previous acquirement of this art the power of forming letters is greatly facilitated, and the time is saved which children lose in correcting bad habits contracted by the practice of bad writing.

The elements of geometry were included under the head of Form, and Pestalozzian instructors have been as successful in this science as in that of number. We will extract from a Preface by Dr. Mayo, to a work entitled " Lessons on Form," an account of the manner of treating this subject :—

In the choice and adoption of Form as a subject of instruction and a means of education, Pestalozzi exhibited as much sagacity as he did in seizing hold of arithmetic and turning it to these purposes. " Bacon observes," says Dr. Mayo, "that a man really possesses only that knowledge which he in some degree creates for himself. To apply to intellectual instruction the principle implied in these words was the aim of Pestalozzi. It is a principle admitting of various degrees, as well as modes of application, in the different branches of human knowledge; but in no one can it be more extensively applied than in geometry. That science is peculiarly the creation of the human mind, in which, independent of external nature, and complete in its own resources, it builds up the solid

but airy fabric of its abstractions. It needs no labora
tory to test its conclusions, no observatory to obtain
data for its calculations ; rendering aid to other
sciences, it asks none for itself.

" Hence, that teacher will act most in conformity
with the genuine character of the science, and consequently will render the study of it the most interesting
and the most improving, who invites and trains his
pupils to create the largest portion of it for themselves.
In geometry, the master must not dogmatize, either in
his own person or through the medium of his book ;
but he must lead his pupils to observe, to determine,
to demonstrate for themselves. In order to accomplish this, he must study the intellectual process in the
acquisition of *original* mathematical knowledge ; and
having ascertained what are the conditions of successful investigation, he must so arrange his plan of
instruction as that these conditions may be perfectly
supplied. He cannot fail to perceive that the leading
requisites are a clear apprehension of the subject-
matter, and well-formed habits of mathematical
reasoning. . . . . The master, led by these considerations, will, in directing the first labours of his pupils,
consider it as his especial aim to enable them
to form clear apprehensions of the subject-matter of
geometry, and then to develop the power of mathematical reasoning. Aware that clearness of appre-

hension can take place only when the idea to be formed
is proximate to some idea already clearly formed—
when the step which the mind is required to take is
really the next in succession to the step already taken,
he will commence his instruction exactly at that point
where his pupils already are, and in that manner
which best accords with the measure of their development. As his pupils are unaccustomed to pure
abstractions, he will not commence with abstract
definitions. But supposing them, through the medium
of ' Lessons on Objects,' to have had their attention
directed to the forms which matter assumes, he will
present in his first lessons a transition from the
promiscuous assemblage of forms to a particular
group of them, the regular solids. In conformity
with the plan pursued in ' Lessons on Objects,' the
pupils will examine regular solids presented to them,
state what they perceive ; then, by a more close and
attentive examination, directed by the master, discover and supply the deficiencies in their first perceptions, and afford him an occasion for connecting
their new ideas with adequate technical expressions.

"The master's next aim is to cultivate the power
of abstract mathematical reasoning. With a view to
this end, he may advantageously avail himself of .the
knowledge obtained by the pupils from the solids in
the manner above described. Here, then, he will lead

them to deduce the necessary consequences from the facts which they know to be true, and then invite them to examine the object, and see whether their reasoning has led to a correct result. Thus, if a child has ascertained and knows that two sides of different planes are requisite to form an edge, and that a certain solid (an octahedron) is bounded by eight triangular planes, he will be required to determine from these data the number of edges which that solid has. He will reason thus : Eight triangular faces have twenty-four sides ; two sides form one edge ; therefore, as many times as there are two sides in these twenty-four sides, so many edges that body must have—that is, twelve edges. This result being obtained, the object is presented to him for examination, and he perceives by actual observation the truth of that conclusion at which he had arrived by abstract reasoning.

"These lessons form the basis of the introduction to geometry, and their results are, correct ideas of the subject-matter of the subsequent lessons, adequate expressions for these ideas, and sound knowledge of the definitions, which form the connecting link between physical and abstract truths.

"When the pupils have gone through the elementary course, they are found competent to demonstrate for themselves the greater part of the propositions in Euclid. These advantages arise from the application

226

of a principle generally neglected in early education, but deserving of consideration and universal adoption, namely, that every course of scientific instruction should be preceded by a preparatory course, arranged on psychological principles. First form a mind, then furnish it." *

CONCLUSION.

It is not the object of this little work to enter fully into the details of Pestalozzi's system. A word, however, to objectors. Some, perhaps, will be ready to exclaim, We find but little new in this much-vaunted system; are not these the principles now generally acted upon? To some extent it is so, and this is what we have before stated—that Pestalozzianism has crept into and leavened the education of our land, though it is scarcely known whence the impetus proceeded which has given new life to our institutions

* The "Lessons on Form," by Mr. Charles Reiner, form a beautiful application of these principles. Respecting them Dr. Mayo observes:—"It has been found in the actual use of these Lessons for a considerable period, that a larger average number of pupils are brought to study mathematics with decided success, and that all pursue them in a superior manner. There is much less of mere mechanical committing to memory, of mere otiose admission and comprehension of demonstrations ready-made, and proportionably more of independent judgment and original reasoning. They not only learn mathematics, but they become mathematicians."

and our schools. It is this system which has taught us that reading, writing, and arithmetic do not constitute education—that instruction does not constitute education, nor even intellectual development itself—but that education, to use Pestalozzi's own expression, has to train the hand, the head, and the heart. This, too, is the system which has taught us that the use of signs should not precede the knowledge of the things signified ; that we must place the ladder of knowledge on a firm basis in the child's mind, and proceed from the known to the unknown ; a principle, indeed, which our Lord Himself has recognized in His teaching by parables. Let us grant that Pestalozzi is not to be considered as the discoverer of new principles : yet has he, at least, as the propounder of a system, "the merit of one who says it so long, so loud, and so clearly, that he compels mankind to hear him ; of one who is so deeply impressed with the importance of the discovery, that he will take no denial, but, at the risk of fortune and fame, pushes through all opposition, and is determined that what he thinks he has discovered shall not perish for want of a fair trial."

———

As Model Lessons are so much used in the training of teachers, and Miss Mayo's works mainly consist of these, the following description of her "Lessons on

Shells " is extracted rom Dr. Mayo's Preface to that work. "The end or which these lessons are laid before the public is not that they may serve as an instructive and entertaining volume to be placed in the hands of children, but in order that the subject may be more familiarly handled and more vividly conceived. They represent an imaginary group of pupils conversing and receiving instruction. The object my sister has proposed to herself is to place a volume in the teacher's hands which shall help him to re-act with his pupils the scenes that are here described. It is not a drama offered for perusal in the closet, but a manager's copy commended to the conductors of other theatres of education, to enable their liliputian *corps dramatiques* to assume the same characters, play the same parts, and I will not say, 'fret their little hour upon the stage,' but enjoy the genuine delight of intellectual activity judiciously directed."

Henderson & Spalding, Printers, 3 & 5, Marylebone Lane, London, W.

.

www.ingramcontent.com/pod-product-compliance
Lightning Source LLC
Chambersburg PA
CBHW030316270326
41926CB00010B/1390